1933

10 88

THE
GERMAN REVOLUTION

The
GERMAN REVOLUTION

ITS MEANING AND MENACE

by

JOSEPH KING

With a Preface by

VISCOUNT SNOWDEN

LONDON
WILLIAMS & NORGATE LTD
28–30 LITTLE RUSSELL STREET, W.C.1
1933

To

HELENA

FOR HER
ENCOURAGEMENT, CRITICISM
AND ASSISTANCE

PRINTED IN GREAT BRITAIN BY
UNWIN BROTHERS LIMITED, LONDON AND WOKING

CONTENTS

VI. THE WORLD COLLAPSE. REICHSTAG   43
     OR REVOLUTION?

     Forces Against Labour—Reichstag Government
     Threatened—Reichstag Election of Septem-
     ber 14, 1930—Financial Anxiety Abroad—
     Military Parades—Growth of Turbulence—
     Hoover Moratorium — Disarmament — The
     "Anschluss"

VII.   REICHSTAG   WEAKER.   HITLER
        STRONGER   49

     Conditions of 1931 Favour Hitler—Nazi
     Increase of Votes—Great Events of 1932—
     President Hindenburg—Hindenburg Re-elected
     President—Hindenburg Dismisses Brüning—
     Lausanne Conference—German Withdrawal
     from Disarmament Conference—Hitler's Policy
     —von Schleicher Chancellor—German Claim
     to Equality in Arms—New Year 1933 Opens
     Ominously—Hitler Chancellor

VIII. HITLER: THE MAN AND HIS METHODS   59

     Adolf Hitler—The Nazi Party—Hitler in the
     Munich Putsch—Hitler's Book: "My Struggle"
     —Hitler in Leipzig Court—Hitler's Belief in
     Himself—Hitler as Orator—Hitler in his
     Meetings—Hitler and the Masses—Nazi Publi-
     cations—Nazi Flag and Swastika—Hitler's
     Authority

IX. NAZIS AND NATIONALISTS   71

     Hitler's Cabinet—Von Papen—Von Neurath
     —Hugenberg—Seldte—Schacht—Von Blom-
     berg—Von Krosigk—Gürtner—Rübenaich—
     Nationalist Ministers but Nazi Policy—Göring
     —Goebbels — Frick — Kerrl — Rosenberg —
     Rosenberg's Mission to London—Feder—
     Röhm—The Nazi Prospect

PREFACE

By VISCOUNT SNOWDEN

THE remarkable growth of the Nazi movement in Germany is a phenomenon which few Englishmen are able to understand. The rise to a position of virtual dictatorship of a man who two years ago was not even a German citizen, and whose influence has been derived from the practice of the arts of an agitator and demagogue, seems so inconsistent with the German character and tradition that we must seek an explanation in the political and economic conditions of Germany which Hitler has successfully exploited.

The Nazi movement is by no means confined to the class from which an agitator usually draws his support. Hitler's popularity is as great among the old ruling class as among the intellectual proletariat.

So far as I am aware there has been no book published in England which has examined and set forth Hitlerism in its historical setting. This little volume is an attempt to do that.

The injustices inflicted upon Germany by the terms of the Peace Treaty, the failure of the Great Powers to redress her grievances and to implement their pledges in regard to disarmament, and perhaps as much as anything the economic depression and the closing of opportunities for the educated classes, have made the German people desperate, and responsive to a leader who voiced their feelings and offered a programme of relief.

The Nazi Revolution, like all revolutions, has been accompanied by terrorism and the suppression of freedom of speech and of the press. A revolution cannot permanently establish itself unless it suppresses all counter-revolutionary parties and organizations.

But the Nazi Revolution has carried terrorism and suppression far beyond what seemed to be necessary to maintain its authority. The persecution of the Jews, and the torture which has been inflicted upon them, have aroused intense indignation throughout the world, and alienated a good deal of the friendly feeling towards Germany and sympathy with her grievances.

Germany cannot be indifferent to world opinion, and there are perhaps signs that the rigour of the Terror is being moderated.

If, as the Revolutionary Government gains confidence in its stability, it allows reasonable freedom for all parties and classes, and stops racial persecution, the world will watch with sympathy its experiments in social and economic reconstruction, and especially if it adheres to the foreign policy laid down in Hitler's recent speech.

The writer of this book knows Germany well. He has long been a keen student of German affairs. His book should be widely read in England as it gives an illuminating explanation of a movement of world significance and importance.

THE GERMAN REVOLUTION

CHAPTER I

INTRODUCTORY

REVOLUTIONS overtook the two great Empires of Continental Europe as they fell exhausted in the World War. The old regimes of Russia and Germany went past recall. Russia in 1917 collapsed through War exhaustion and inner corruption; the men who seized power have made the Revolution in Russia a firmly established Government. The German Revolution started in November 1918, when the Kaiser fled for safety to Holland, with an offer of Peace from the enemy; in less than a year it seemed accepted at home and recognized abroad.

Russia, with all the nations against her, fighting and starving, impoverished and outlawed, established an order of things of an absolutely new type, which has lasted fifteen years.

Germany, with a new democratic Weimar Constitution, which seemed democratic, non-military, conciliatory, leading in science, in organized manufacturing and social welfare methods, had a promise of a place in peaceful Europe. Its Revolution has passed into Hitler-

ism of which the meaning and menace must
be faced.

The German Revolution of 1933 follows the
Russian Communist, and the Italian Fascist,
Revolutions; they are each the Dictatorship of
a definite political party. In each the dominant
party deprives all other parties of any voice or
share in Government, preserves for its members
the best paid and most influential offices, uses
complete censorship of the press and publicity,
exercises firm grasp on postal, telephone, tele-
graphic and other services, maintains rigid pass-
port methods, has adopted peculiar methods
and principles of law and Law Courts, exercises
imprisonment without charge, practises "pre-
cautionary" removals of opponents, and makes
acts of terrorism an order of the day.

As in Russia and Italy, so also in Germany,
a great Leader has emerged, a man who by
his iron will, singleness of aim, courage, clear
view of coming events and strong personality,
has become the hero of his party and has stood
for his nation in the eyes of the world. To-day
Mussolini rules in Rome as much an autocrat
as Caesar Augustus, and more beloved. Hitler
wields in Berlin a power greater than any
power ever possessed by Bismarck or Kaiser,
and is adored and obeyed by his party as no
previous Ruler in Germany. Is Hitler's future
to follow the lines of the Dictatorships in
Russia and Italy?

CHAPTER II

THE ALLIES AND THE REVOLUTION

The Armistice—Peace Conference in Paris—Terms of the Peace—Conferences of the Allies—Reparations —Military Occupation in Rhineland—The Ruhr— Rhineland High Commission—Refugees—"Separatists"—Good Will at Last!

THE ARMISTICE

In November 1918 the President of the United States negotiated with Erzberger and other leading Germans to grant an Armistice, promising Peace on the basis of his famous Fourteen Points, which offered a reasonable basis of future good will and a pacified Europe. Relying on the Fourteen Points, Germany capitulated. "Only the Fourteen Points" was a slogan heard in Germany long after the War.

By the Armistice conditions, war material, guns, arms, ships, submarines, transport vehicles, railway engines, aeroplanes, stores, etc., had to be immediately surrendered; the object was to make it impossible for Germany to renew hostilities if Peace Terms were not agreed upon. The German Armies still on Foreign soil retreated in disorder and despair to their homes; the blockade of Germany on all sides by the Allies prevented all raw materials and all foods from entering the country, even from lands which up to the Armistice had been able to send supplies. Numbers of the German population died as direct offerings to the Blockade, especially young children and aged persons.

PEACE CONFERENCE AT PARIS

The Peace Conference began at Paris, a huge gathering of the "Allies and Associated Powers" with their experts and influential men of all classes and countries, who had, or hoped to get, gains or profits out of the years of the War; it was brought to a conclusion after weeks of wrangling over the spoils and fruits of victory; the Peace Treaty was made.

Threatened with continued and intensified starvation and the advance of the Allies to the heart of disarmed Germany, the Peace of Versailles was signed on June 28, 1919.

TERMS OF THE PEACE

The Treaty of Peace, dictated to Germany, not mutually agreed to by German negotiators, contained many heavy penalties. Among these:

Territorial Losses of Germany by the Peace:—
    Alsace-Lorraine to France.
    Great Provinces in the East, predominately German in majority, to Poland, including
    Silesia in part (against result in Plebiscite);
    Danzig, made Free City, with Poland having certain Sovereign Rights over it;
    Strips to Denmark, Belgium, Czechoslovakia;
    Saar District to France, to exploit its rich coal and iron for fifteen years.

The German Army and Navy limited to 100,000, with no conscription or short service, limited as to arms, no big guns, no tanks, no aircraft, submarines, ships limited in number, tonnage, size of guns, etc.

Western Districts towards France to be held by Allied Armies for fifteen years, and the cost of providing for the Enemy Armies paid by Germany (3 Occupied Zones).

Reparations to the Allies were imposed by the Treaty to an unnamed amount, but in respect of various categories, one of which was Payment of Pensions, which had been definitely excluded in the Armistice Terms; £1,000,000,000 named in Treaty as first payment.

The Trial of the Kaiser, which the British Premier made the first of his General Election aims in 1918, was never seriously intended or proposed; the demand to punish German "War Criminals" was attempted till the cases tried at Leipzig collapsed by their weakness; economic conditions imposed to keep poor the country from which the Allies were demanding immense sums.

It was a dictated Peace made in the spirit of revenge; to obtain aggrandizement for the Victors and the political and economic enfeeblement of the Vanquished.

The Peace handed to the Germans needed courage for them to sign. The men who signed it for Germany, and afterwards were forced by the Allies to carry it out, knew that it was made to impoverish their country and feared it would bring them the reproach of their countrymen.

CONFERENCES OF THE ALLIES

The Peace formalities out of the way, the Allied Statesmen began the long series of Conferences at which they claimed that they were establishing the world on better lines. From 1918 International Conferences have formed one of the standing features of World Affairs.

The Conference of Spa in July 1920, eighth of the Allied Conferences, was the first time when German Ministers met the Allied Statesmen on a formal equal footing. It concerned itself with the Disarmament of Germany and the deliveries of coal as Reparations in kind; it was typical of the relations which existed for the first five years of the Peace—Germany pleading against her crushing burdens, the Allies using military threats to press their demands.

REPARATIONS

Two conditions of the Peace, apart from the other hardships, explain why a peaceful, contented, and conciliatory Germany was impossible in the years 1918–23. These are the demand for Reparations to an unlimited amount and the Military Occupation of the Rhineland.

Reparations have now been paid enough to repair much of the material damage done. But they have caused bitterness, disappointment and disillusion. Planned to continue for sixty years, they are a thing of the past, in thirteen years given up as irrecoverable debts.

MILITARY OCCUPATION IN RHINELAND

The facts of the Occupied Areas must be still remembered. To the Germans they meant great losses and humiliation, material and moral, and memories of gross ill-treatment. Hitler never fails to recall them.

THE RUHR

In 1922, dissatisfied with German payments, the French Premier, Poincaré, determined to invade the rich iron and coal district, the Ruhr, with its huge works of Krupp, Thyssen and others; he proposed to seize, manage and get the whole profits from the Ruhr mines, furnaces and workshops. On January 11, 1923, the invasion began; the French with tanks, heavy artillery, and a complete Division fully equipped marched into the Ruhr. They maintained their Forces there with constant additions for more than eighteen months. At the end of the first year the Inter-Allied Rhineland Commission reported that hundreds of Germans had been killed, that fines amounting to over £20,000,000 (at par) had been imposed, that all the local Mayors and Railway Officials had been deported, and that nearly

150,000 of the inhabitants had been removed. It was War on a totally unarmed people. Works, offices, Banks, dwellings, public buildings had been seized, and the whole district lived in want of the necessities of life.

The Germans had from the first adopted the policy of Passive Resistance. To resist by force was plainly impossible, but it was possible to say, "Let us leave the Robbers to take what they can get; we shall not desert the people of the Ruhr; we can send the workers there enough to keep them from want and starvation."

The French were none the richer for the first year's occupation; they went into the second year of the Ruhr enterprise with sterner methods; their rule in the Occupied Area became more ruthless and intolerable; schools were requisitioned and 130,000 children turned out of doors. Two hundred newspapers were stopped issue or importation; private citizens were robbed in the streets; the American Inspector of the Y.M.C.A. reported on "the Reign of Terror," which he found on his visit.

RHINELAND HIGH COMMISSION

The proceedings of the Allies in the Occupied Area were dictated by the Inter-Allied Rhineland High Commission, a body arising out of the formal agreement by which Germany recognized the right to occupy parts of her territory. On it were representatives originally of Germany, U.S.A., and Britain, as well as of France and Belgium. It became the autocratic engine of French militarism. When the Ruhr Campaign was planned, it was France in complete control, being supported by Belgium, with the British Representative in a minority of one on any vital issues (U.S.A. and Germany being withdrawn).

The rule of French Soldiers in the Ruhr was to be closely repeated ten years later by the Brown Shirt soldiers of Hitler in Berlin. Each made a Reign of Terror.

The Inter-Allied High Commission ruled the occupied Rhineland with cruel coarseness; continually asking for new buildings for Officers, their families, and their Clubs, bringing in Spahis, and African black troops whose manners and habits offended the population; thousands of German civilians were sent to prison for infringing arbitrary regulations changed or imposed with sudden surprises; fines, often heavy for what seemed trivial breaches of rules, were freely imposed.

REFUGEES

In Unoccupied Germany there were thousands of refugees from their homes and businesses in Ruhr and Rhineland, unemployed, impoverished, with incredible stories to tell. Men were becoming accustomed to violence. Its sight and practice were so familiar that it was copied. It became natural to attempt violence, if counsel and conciliation did not succeed.

SEPARATISTS

The French made efforts to set up a Separatist "Autonomous Republic" in the Rhineland. This scheme promoted treachery to the German Republic. Nominally France and Germany were at peace, had been so for three years, and diplomatic relations and normal communications between the two Powers continued. Yet French officers were supporting traitorous actions and subversive plans, restraining the German Police in their efforts to stop the sedition. It was only because British newspapers like *The Times* and *Manchester Guardian*, and British Officers and Diplomatists, stood with courage for decent fair play that the Separatist Conspiracy was crushed. The German populace and police with fire and bloodshed finished off the bands of jail-birds, criminals, dissolute and misguided fellows, to whom the French had supplied arms, money, protection, special free travel and publicity facilities. Arson, murder, robbery, assault and kidnapping, seizing public offices, had been the savage practices of the Separatists. These things had been done on German soil in 1923 by foreigners with criminal intent. They furnished a model and a forecast of what Germans could do on a larger scale in 1933.

GOOD WILL AT LAST!

A new prospect arose and an evil period closed
when in 1924 changes of Government came in
Britain and France, "substituting co-operation
and good will for force as the motive in con-
temporary diplomacy."

CHAPTER III

THE REPUBLIC AND ITS OBSTACLES

*Republic Never got Fair Play—Privileged Opponents—
Hugo Stinnes—Reichstag Started Weak—The Reichswehr — The Kapp Putsch — Reactionary Judges—
Ebert, First President—Erzberger—Military Clubs
and Private Armies*

REPUBLIC NEVER GOT FAIR PLAY

THE German Revolution of November 1918 and its Weimar Constitution of May 1919 never had a fair chance from nations abroad nor from its own citizens. For five years after the War by the Peace Conditions the Great Powers treated Germany without patience, reason, humanity and attempts at reconciliation. The new States on the East, especially Poland, faced her with threatening military forces. Republican Germany was feeble in diplomacy; she had been held unworthy to be given a seat in the League of Nations, of which Haiti and Liberia were among the original Members. Junker Barons would not take part in the democratic Republic, demanded by the victors and "fashioned" by professors, lawyers, tradesmen and trades unionists at Weimar.

The present writer recalls conversation with Germans ten years ago when, after enjoying the hospitality of their table, he was told, "We can suffer our defeat, after four years fighting against the rest of Europe, Asia and America; but Germany can and shall be great again; not under these democrats, who think that by submission and trying to carry out an impossible Treaty they can become your friends in a peaceful Europe; that is against the spirit and the great traditions of Germany." When on a later occasion the writer was where the conversation led to the assassinations of Erzberger and Rathenau, he said, "What a loss it is when really great men, who are known and respected abroad and show character and courage at home, are killed by cowardly assassins! and how strange to us that the murderers are allowed to get away!" The reply he got was, "Well, you cannot expect us to regret that these men were *done in*. I certainly do not wish the keen young Germans who did it to be condemned."

The New Democratic Republic never got a fair deal from the Monarchist party, whose wealth, influence, newspapers, plots and propaganda, often illegal and always intentionally subversive, prevented it gaining the respect and success it deserved.

PRIVILEGED OPPONENTS

If the Military Caste, the Landlords and the Officials of the Higher Class were no friends of the new Republic, they retained their pensions, properties, their titles and many privileges; the Kaiser and his family retained their huge wealth, and were never in danger of life nor of the malignant slander to which the new leaders of the Republic were subject. The great Industrialists and Financiers were

ready to wreck the Republic of the pacifists
and the workers, if their profits and businesses
were saved.

HUGO STINNES

Hugo Stinnes was famous in Germany and Europe as
a man of great wealth, controlling numerous undertakings and industries, especially those connected with
steel and iron, coal and transport in Rhineland and
Western Europe. He was a cruel foe of the new Republic
and used every means to evade the obligations of the
Peace Treaty.

"Stinnes, the father of German Trusts, the inventor
of that unholy partnership, between owners and workmen to exploit the consumers, that resulted in the social
disintegration of Germany, the representative of German
imperialism at its most brutal, who could not distinguish
politics from his private ends (he took 'brokerage profits
on deliveries in kind' to the Allies). The partisan of
inflation, who invented the plan of circumventing reparation payments by a 'cheap bankruptcy' that would
transfer property intact from the German State to the
rich industrialists. The masterly financier, who destroyed
his enemies without respect for weapons, refused to pay
his taxes, rose uninvited at the Spa Conference (he was
not even a delegate) and hurled his defiance in the face
of the Allied representatives. The ruthless schemer who
dared the French to enter the Ruhr, organized passive
resistance against them, but, when it began to hurt, was
the first to demand its cessation—and got away with the
loot, sharing it with the French. 'Overbearing, wrong-
headed and inclined to insolence,' as Lord D'Abernon
described him. The predatory being, whose spirit never
recovered from the blow of having to submit to the
French, Hugo Stinnes, for years the real ruler and evil
genius of Germany." (E. A. Mowrer, *Germany Puts the
Clock Back*, p. 57.)

REICHSTAG STARTED WEAK

Germany, having accepted defeat in War and made a new regime with a new written Constitution, endorsed by the masses of the people and welcomed even abroad, still made a bad start with the Reichstag. The strong Conservatism in State and big business remained, as has been described, crippled but hostile; sullen but constantly on the watch to discredit their new politics, Stinnes in the business world and Ludendorff in the military ranks were ready to be traitors to the State.

The Weimar Republic was a failure and its democratic leaders never learned to lead a nation.

THE REICHSWEHR

The Reichswehr, the limited Army of 100,000, which the Peace Treaty forced Germany to maintain, was from the first a reactionary menace; it was led and organized by men of the old military caste; it helped the secret retention of arms which the Allies sought to discover; it insisted on secrecy from the popular eye; it made preparations in Russia and formed illicit connections there and elsewhere to provide for future military possibilities.

THE KAPP PUTSCH

In March 1920 the Putsch made by Kapp, excellently arranged and carried out from a military point of view, would have succeeded in restoring the Monarchy and destroying the Reichstag had not a general strike of the Workers started in Berlin at once; then the plot was a burst bubble. It was not the Reichswehr, nor the police, nor the Reichstag and its politicians, but the Workers that saved the State. Officers and officials who joined in with Kapp were let off and reinstated.

The writer was in 1922 discussing things in Germany with a well-disposed retired officer of the Kaiser's Army, who maintained against criticisms of the great cost, the extravagant ideas and aims of the force, that, though restricted in equipment and otherwise, the Reichswehr was to be "the best fighting army in the world for its efficiency and training." He held that the British had just given a freedom to Ireland and had made promises of freedom to Egypt, because their lands had "shown fight"; "Neither Ireland nor Egypt could attack, still less invade England, and yet England gave way; we in Germany must make our Reichswehr a force to be respected."

REACTIONARY JUDGES

Another grave obstacle to the position of the new Republic existed in the Courts of Law and especially the Criminal Courts. The Judges were those of the old regime, largely from the families and circles with old royalist prejudices. Their injustices and surprising sentences would fill a volume. Arising out of the Kapp Putsch, a workman who shot a mutinous rebel received fifteen years' penal servitude (at that time Capital Punishment had not been reimposed), while rebellious soldiers in Thuringia, who shot down workmen, were acquitted.

EBERT, FIRST PRESIDENT

There was no effort of the Republican Reichstag to mitigate this old Prussianism. The stubborn persistence of Militarism in activity was never really met, though it was always evident. The first Minister of Defence,

Noske, was a Social-Democrat. Ebert, the first President, whose portrait on postage stamps has been an offence to Hitler, and whose son has been thrashed by the Brown Shirts because he is not ashamed of his dead parent—Ebert was by no means a pacifist, he had voted in the Reichstag for the War Credits and supported the prosecution of the war till the victory was evidently going to Germany's enemies—Ebert, a plain straightforward typical German, who, when the power "had slipped from the hands of the nerveless generals, snatched it from the street where the Communists were about to seize it, and handed it back to the generals." Why? "Through patriotism; through fear of Communism; through abhorrence of disorder; through the deference owned by 'the lower orders' to their social superiors" (Mowrer, p. 70).

ERZBERGER

Matthias Erzberger was only twenty-eight years of age when he was elected to the Reichstag in 1875, as a member of the Catholic Centre; he soon established fame by his grasp and criticism of financial questions, and by his exposure of financial scandals in the Colonial Office in which persons of high social position were implicated; during the War he was active in German propaganda among Catholics abroad; he led the famous Reichstag movement in July 1918 in favour of Germany accepting peace "without annexations"; and he led the German negotiations for an Armistice; when the Peace Treaty was imposed on Germany and no alteration, consideration or amendment admitted, when the Allied Ultimatum of July 19, 1919, offered either full acceptance or renewed war, he saw that this meant chaos for Germany, offered the Generals to retire if they could resume the fight, on their declining to answer, he took the lead, though not the Chancellorship, when a new Government started the severe duty of carrying out the Peace Treaty. Erzberger was the political genius of the early Republican period; personally aggressive and without charm and the tactful ways essential to a great

leader, his quick and right decisions in crises, his prompt
actions, driving power and unfailing resource made him
able to dominate Governments in which he was in not
the official head. He unified the Reich finances; he taxed
the rich financiers and profiteers; he was libelled, slan-
dered and abused as no other Republican and reformer
ever was in Germany; he was foully murdered in
August 1921 by youths instigated by secret reactionary
organizations.

MILITARY CLUBS AND PRIVATE ARMIES

The story of the revival of the military state
lies not only in the doings of the Reichswehr,
but in Clubs, Societies, Old Comrades,
"Fronts," which grew into armed bands and
"private Armies." The most reputable, largest
and oldest was the Stahlhelm (Steel-helmets).
The variety of these bodies is baffling; some
were violent and criminal, like the black
Reichswehr which accounted for the murders
of Erzberger and Rathenau. "Private armies"
arose, armed with clubs or sticks, but often
and increasingly with revolvers and army
weapons; these plain civilians came not merely
to play at soldiering and to prevent risings or
outrages. The *Reichsbanner*, the great Republican organization, came later; it was declared
illegal in 1932 by von Papen, when the Brown
Shirts were legalized. No strong line was drawn
against these organized "private armies." They
were tolerated because there were too many
disbanded soldiers and starving desperate men
on the streets: they multiplied in numbers, in

arms and in defiance of the civil power; they had been a disturbing factor, they became a grave danger and they ended by making the Revolution a military dictatorship. The Brown Shirt Army of Hitler has now swallowed up whatever of the other private armies it has not destroyed.

CERTAIN GERMAN EXPRESSIONS

In these pages certain German words are used as being well understood; e.g. Kaiser, Reich, Junker (landed aristocrat), and Putsch (an abortive armed insurrection).

The "Brown Shirts," now playing in Germany a part like the black-shirt Fascisti in Italy, are spoken of, when formally referred to, as S.A. = Sturm Abteilungen, Storm Detachments. They are distinct from the Nazi S.S., an élite force; S.S. = Schutz Staffel, Guard Squads.

CHAPTER IV

GERMANY'S EFFORT TO PAY

Political Parties—The Communists—Rathenau—The
Ruhr and Inflation—Stresemann—Inflation Collapse
Before the Ruhr—The Dawes Plan

POLITICAL PARTIES

POLITICAL parties in the Reichstag have their
basis in the social layers of German society. On
the extreme right sit the Nazis; then the
Nationalists, based on the old Junker families
and their class; in the next tier of seats is the
German People's Party, the superior people,
the Big Business men, the party based on the
commercial class; the Centre Party (Zentrum)
is Catholic in its basic elements; within it are
groups, strongly reactionary and also democratic peasants and workers; this Catholic
Centre has been true to Parliamentary rights
and has joined with the parties next on its
left in the coalitions which have upheld the
efforts of Parliamentary Rule. The Democrats
are the party of the reformers, heirs of the old
Liberalism after 1848, largely professional and
cultured men of the cities, based on intellect
and education. Then come what was till 1932
for years the largest party in the Reichstag, the
Social-Democrats based on the organized and
class-conscious workers, mostly trade unionists,

with many of the lower middle class. The
Democrats, Centre and Socialists are the three
Parties, all loyal to the German Nation in the
War and after it, Republican, anti-monarchical,
believing in Parliamentary Government and
Peace abroad, and they might have maintained
the Revolution as a moderate Parliamentary
system if they had kept together, and if they
had been content to drop or delay their
special party programmes and sectional aims.

THE COMMUNISTS

The extreme Left on the Reichstag tiers is
occupied by the Communists, the party of
workers whose internationalism is the ortho-
dox creed of Marx, taking their inspiration and
orders from Russia. The Communists have
been in constant bitter antagonism to the
Social-Democrats, with whom they could unite
against taxation impositions on the workers,
but not in making a united front against
Nationalists and Nazis. They united in the
Street in 1920, in the General Strike that ended
at once the Kapp Putsch. A similar united
effort of Social-Democrat and Communist
forces would have prevented the Revolution of
the Nazis in 1933.

The Communists were never strong enough
to follow the violent seizure of power which
had succeeded in Russia. Encouraged from
Moscow to aim at this, they found most

German workers only fitfully inclined to it. They never had commanding leaders in the nation or Reichstag. Their polling strength, always great, has varied and often caused trouble, especially in Saxony, but represented the most depressed and desperate class of poor workers in the towns. To the reactionaries they have been invaluable as a plausible and ever-repeated proof that Communism was *The Danger*, and they are to the Nazi movement to-day the unending theme of the destruction, from which Hitler has saved not only Germany but Western Civilization.

RATHENAU

Walter Rathenau became Foreign Secretary in the Cabinet of Dr. Wirth in October 1921; he had already made his mark as Minister of Reconstruction; he had met the Frenchman, Loucheur, and by the Wiesbaden Agreement had given confidence that Germany would keep her promise to restore the ravaged region of France. In the War he had done notable work in organizing supplies and distribution in the German War Office. Rathenau was at once an artist, author, philosopher, scientist, linguist, and head of the great Electrical Combine, A.E.G. At the Genoa Conference he had played a leading rôle, supporting Lloyd George against Poincaré in an effort to start a new European policy of appeasement. He made and announced, perhaps prematurely, the Treaty of Rapallo with Russia. Three months later he was murdered by a fanatic youth instigated by a secret reactionary gang as he drove through the streets of Berlin.

THE RUHR AND INFLATION

A non-party Cabinet under Cuno was formed in November 1922 to face the threatened Invasion of the Ruhr by the French. The threat united the most opposed elements of the Nation, against this renewal of War, after the German efforts to pay Reparations. The injustice and "trumpery" excuse for the French Invasion had been denounced by Sir John Bradbury, the British representative on the Reparation Commission. The policy of Germany to meet French force by Passive Resistance meant that to support the sufferers in the Ruhr the Government could only go on printing notes with no security to support them.

STRESEMANN

The way was led in November 1923 to an effort to get again into negotiations with France. At this point Stresemann became Foreign Secretary, in November 1923. This was the opening of a new phase for Germany. How was the catastrophic fall of the Mark to be got over? How was the progressive Inflation to be replaced by a stable Currency? The task seemed impossible. The demands of the Allies for Reparations were crushing. The claims of both Labour and Capital were insatiable. Yet a new currency, based on immovable resources, was created by the Rentenbank, and was established on Gold.

INFLATION COLLAPSE BEFORE THE RUHR

The historic Inflation of German currency, which proceeded till the Mark was worthless, began with the pressing demand for Reparations between April 1921 and the Ruhr occupation in 1923.

The War had been financed by Germany much more by borrowing than by taxation, and by issues of loans to which the people of the German middle classes mostly subscribed. The Reparation Demands produced the disastrous fall of the Mark. This fall was completed by the Ruhr policy. The unbending attitude of both sides, French and German, refusing compromise in a bitter trial of endurance, meant for both countries collapse of the currency. Germany impoverished her middle classes, the rentiers, completely, but was able to start afresh with the Rentenmark, at the same par value as the pre-war Mark, 20 marks to the Pound. France, by the efforts of Poincaré, who had led the policy which depreciated the franc, induced the French Chamber to establish the currency on the basis of 125 francs to the pound.

THE DAWES PLAN

The dawn on Germany broke when a change of Government in France and Germany led to the appointment of Two Committees of Experts. On their Reports the Dawes Plan for the payment of Reparations was formed. General Dawes, the U.S.A. expert, was Chairman of the Committee to consider how Germany could balance

her budget and stabilize her currency; he has acknowledged the outstanding part in his Plan taken by Sir
Josiah Stamp, the British representative. Mr. Reginald
McKenna presided over the other Committee. Long
negotiations followed the issue of their recommendations.
The difficulties were great, but doubts were dispelled and
suspicions relieved. On August 30, 1924, the London
Agreements were signed. Germany was free to raise without interference the sums she agreed to pay. The Dawes
German Loan was raised, by issues in London, Paris
and Brussels, and was eagerly subscribed. The financial
world now saw that Germany had a stable currency
and could be trusted to pay her debts.

CHAPTER V

STRESEMANN AND COMPLIANCE

Stresemann Offers a Peace Pact—Germany and the League—Stresemann's Achievements—The Treaty of Locarno—Germany's Admission to the League—Locarno Opposed by Reactionaries—Recovery After Locarno—The Hague Conference, 1929. The Young Plan—Military Occupation Ended

STRESEMANN OFFERS A PEACE PACT

"JANUARY 20, 1925, should be written in golden letters in the history of post-War Europe." These words are used by Lord D'Abernon of the day on which Stresemann laid before the British Government his proposal for a Pact by which Germany should agree with France and with Britain for the mutual maintenance of Peace in Europe. Stresemann's policy placed his country in such an improved political and economic condition that the recovery of Germany's power in Europe was in prospect.

GERMANY AND THE LEAGUE

The Dawes Plan, accepted by the Powers on August 30, 1924, gave diplomatic, if not political, freedom to Germany. The question of Germany entering the League of Nations came up. France was suspicious; Britain was careful not to offend France; Briand was always, to the end of his life, held back by the strong nationalistic forces in the French Chamber. On the German side, there was no strong support for the League of Nations; it was widely held that the League was started as a League of Victors, and so remained. The Nationalistic elements in Germany were ready to approve, and even arrange, to end Stresemann as they had ended the lives of Erzberger and Rathenau. Stresemann knew that his life was threatened; he was under constant police protection.

STRESEMANN'S ACHIEVEMENTS

Stresemann has to his credit three great events:

The Dawes Settlement of 1924.
The Locarno Agreements of 1925.
Germany's entry in the League of Nations in 1926.

In building these "pillars of peace" others took shares of the work, which required conciliation, patience, persistent faith and efforts. The names of MacDonald, Austen Chamberlain, Herriot and Briand must be remembered honourably. The good results for Germany, though denied by the voice of Hitler, are acclaimed by the rest of the civilized world.

The Dawes Settlement made Germany master in her own house over taxation and administrative control and free from the fiscal and other demands from the Allies which had weakened every Government since 1919. It led also to the speedy Evacuation of the Ruhr and the liberation of its great industries from the exploiting grasp of French capitalist forces, and to improved conduct by the Occupying Armies in the Rhineland. The costs of the Occupation were now much reduced, payments for the armies being reckoned as a set-off against Reparation demands.

The efforts of French Generals and Politicians to help Separatism, the break-away of frontier regions in Germany, and thus to dismember Germany further, were brought to an end.

THE TREATY OF LOCARNO

Stresemann put forward his proposals for new Franco-German relations in January 1925; and on October 16, 1925, the Locarno Agreements were signed by the Ministers of Britain, France, Germany and Belgium. In them the present frontiers are guaranteed; resort to force is in every form renounced; the League of Nations accepted as arbiter in disputes; France thus assured of holding Alsace-Lorraine; Britain though not a Continental Power guaranteeing the other signatories' rights. For the sake of peace and international amity Germany here renounced what to the German reactionary was the cherished hope of the future, a war of revenge. But the faith and courage of Stresemann carried his country to envisage a new Germany.

GERMANY'S ADMISSION TO THE LEAGUE

The signing of the Locarno Treaty was followed by the admission of Germany to Membership of the League of Nations. After some delays, the League Assembly on September 10, 1926, gave an ovation to Stresemann and the German Delegates. Briand roused enthusiasm when he said: "Messieurs, la paix, c'est la signification de ce jour—pour l'Allemagne et la France, cela veut dire; c'est fini, la série de rencontres douloureuses et sanglantes, dont toutes les pages de l'histoire sont tachées dans le passé; c'est fini la guerre entre nous."

A few days later came the famous private luncheon with Briand at Thoiry, heralded by the press before, and much debated and variously judged afterwards. The two friends left Geneva together. Eluding pressmen and publicity they lunched at a country inn, discussing what might still be done to bring France and Germany into close accord. Could they solve outstanding problems?

LOCARNO OPPOSED BY REACTIONARIES

The Treaty of Locarno was accomplished by Stresemann against great opposition at home; it placed the future of Franco-German relations, especially of the Alsace-Lorraine problem, in an entirely new position; by renouncing solutions by force of arms Stresemann brought on himself the rancour and hatred of the reactionaries: the Reichstag ratified, but Berlin Society cursed the Treaty. How he returned from Locarno is described by his biographer (A. Vallentin, *Stresemann*, pp. 190 f.):

"One man and one man only had brought himself and his people out of the deepest valley of defeat on to the world plain of national self-respect.

"He had to face the most violent storm of his stormy experience when he returned to his own country. The Treaty of Locarno was high treason; loud were the shouts for his impeachment that went up from the Press of the Right. The signatories of the Versailles Treaty had at least the excuse that they acted under durance; but Gustav Stresemann, the Traitor, had of his own free will surrendered Alsace-Lorraine to France. He was paid by the French—Frau Stresemann was sister of Madame Poincaré—just as it was once reported that Rathenau's sister had married Radek. Moreover, Stresemann had been bought by the Jews, bribed by the wise men of Zion. This was not merely said, but believed, and that not only in Pomerania and the *Miesbacher Anzieger*, not only in country villages and Old Comrades' Associations, but in Berlin and Dresden; not only by the die-hards of the old regime, but even by the length and breadth of the German middle-class. A flood of filth and slander burst over the head of the returning Minister. He read the first Press comments in the train to Berlin, and a flame of anger flashed into his face. He was so sensitive against criticism that every attack, every vile malignant word, struck him like the lash of a whip.

"The railway station in Berlin was surrounded by police. The hour of his arrival was kept strictly secret; only the heads of foreign missions, who had been confidentially informed of it, were there to meet him. Foreign diplomatists congratulated Stresemann on his great work. His greeting in Germany was indignation and abuse. Lord D'Abernon, a towering figure in his great cloak, shook his hand with singular emotion, and the smile that seemed almost engraved upon his face was for once absent. This quite unemotional personage knew that the weary man who got out of the train had made history. . . . Gustav Stresemann had to enter his native city by devious ways and under police supervision."

At the end of 1926 the Nobel Prize for Peace

was awarded to Stresemann; he went to Oslo to receive it and delivered a speech which was a manifesto of "the New Germany." His health began to fail and his activities bore heavily upon him till the Hague Conference of 1929 broke him down. He returned thence to Berlin to find violent opponents joined in an effort to defeat the work of the Hague Conference. Hugenberg and Hitler had launched a drive to obtain signatures to a petition, which under the Constitution would secure the submission of a "Law against War Guilt and the Young Plan" to a Referendum of the Nation. The drafted Law condemned as Traitors to extreme penalties those who with Stresemann had opened the way for the New Germany. Its authors failed to get sufficient signatures in support. Stresemann, a weakened man, died suddenly on October 3, 1929.

RECOVERY AFTER LOCARNO

The astonishing recovery of Germany since the War has been largely due to the loans made to Germany when the Stresemann policy restored her to a place in peaceful Europe.

The keynote of Stresemann's policy was compliance with the existing conditions; by negotiation and conciliation, by tactful approach and reasonable concession he gained the esteem and respect of Europe; he and Briand the advocates at the League of Nations of a new outlook and a better prospect for Disarmament and Peace.

THE HAGUE CONFERENCE, 1929. THE YOUNG PLAN

The Dawes Settlement of 1924 gave to Germany the right to claim a further revision of the Reparation Payments. This led to the Conference at The Hague, held in August 1929, where two further advantages were given to Germany; the payments were reduced and placed on a new basis and with conditions for meeting unexpected difficulties. This was the Young Plan, under which a new German Loan was raised internationally; the Loan was a great success issued at 5 per cent.

MILITARY OCCUPATION ENDED

The Hague Conference also concluded the Military Occupation of German territory as arranged by the Commission presided over by Mr. Arthur Henderson. The British troops were withdrawn forthwith. The costs of the occupation ceased and for the troops of France and Belgium no more was paid. Accordingly, four years before the date appointed under the Versailles Treaty, the last French soldiers left Germany on June 30, 1930. National rejoicings marked the event, which his country owed to Stresemann: he had died the previous October and did not live to see the day which his Statesmanship had gained.

CHAPTER VI

THE WORLD COLLAPSE. REICHSTAG OR REVOLUTION

Forces Against Labour—Reichstag Government Threatened—Reichstag Election of September 14, 1930—Financial Anxiety Abroad—Military Parades —Growth of Turbulence—Hoover Moratorium— Disarmament—The "Anschluss"

FORCES AGAINST LABOUR

FROM 1929 to 1931 economic and industrial distress produced conditions of increasing danger. German Labour, hopelessly divided between the Social-Democrats, the Centre and the Communists, was made weaker by the growth of unemployment; real wages were now no higher than before the War; Capital's profits were larger. Strengthened by the foreign loans now pressed on them, big business men learned how to avoid taxation, obtain tariffs, subventions and trade privileges, made monopolies, combines and cartels, got free from mortgages, piled up reserves, got improved plant and practised rationalization so well that between 1926 and 1931 it accounted for a million fewer hands required in German factories.

REICHSTAG GOVERNMENT THREATENED

The end of a Parliamentary regime was heralded by two events in the end of 1930, by the beginning of

Emergency Power Degrees and by the Reichstag Election shock of September 14, 1930.

In July 1930, the Coalition Cabinet of Müller had resigned, and Dr. Brüning with another Coalition had failed to get support for his policy of severe taxation; he obtained from President Hindenburg, using the Emergency Powers of Article 48 of the Constitution, the prorogation of the Reichstag and the use of Decrees in place of normal Reichstag law. This method of government came into force in November 1930. Since that date Reichstag has existed only to approve or endorse the Degrees, which are to-day the only legislation known to Germany!

In the course of this change came the Reichstag Election of September 14, 1930. The Result was a surprising proof of the growth of extreme proposals in the people's mind:

Social-Democrats	8,575,200
Nazis	6,406,400
Communists	4,590,200
Centre (Catholics)	4,127,000
Nationalists	2,457,700

Five other parties polled over a million votes each, showing the variety and confusion of policies. Especially alarming was the great vote obtained by the extreme parties to Right (Nazis) and Left (Communists), 13,000,000 voters who favoured a Dictatorship rather than an efficient Reichstag.

FINANCIAL ANXIETY ABROAD

The significance of this election was soon shown in the anxiety, even panic, which induced the creditors of Germany to call in loans; many private loans, at short notice, had to be repaid. When the run to withdraw from Banks and businesses started, it was a serious thing for

Germany; unemployment, trade decline, fiscal
difficulties—all were much aggravated.

MILITARY PARADES

This fateful election indicated how successful
the use of military parades of private bands and
party uniforms and warlike-looking processions
could be. At first many, perhaps most, of those
seeing and taking part in these demonstrations
never had any idea of the use of violence in
party warfare. But from 1930 with the Nazi
storm troops, the Brown Shirt detachments,
terrorizing and stopping at nothing, using
bludgeons and firearms against their fellow-
citizens of other parties, it was civil war at
election times. The police and the authorities
struggled to stop or control this warfare of the
party bands. But too many party leaders
emulated Hitler's instigations to force and
brutality. Nazis were the chief inventors of
this national fashion; it was too strong to be
crushed. It grew till it was an essential to the
exercise of the citizen's rights.

GROWTH OF TURBULENCE

Parades and demonstrations are recognized
and popular in any land where law and order
are observed in public places. But when the
essence is no longer in the order, numbers and
unity of the persons parading, but in the
military equipment of those taking part and

in their menace and challenge, then another
state of things arises. Then clashes and counter-
marches begin. What followed naturally is told
by Mowrer (*Germany Puts the Clock Back*,
Chap. XXII).

"During nearly two years, throughout the most intellectual of European countries . . . not a week passed without
political murders. Not a night without a clash between
National-Socialists and Republicans. Furious fights
between organized political gangs were commonplace,
the weapons being fists, sticks, blackjacks, brass knuckles,
knives, revolvers, hand-grenades, occasionally rifles and
bombs. Jews, Communists, Socialists, Republicans were
subject to regular assassination and (excepting the Jews)
defended themselves in kind. There were dead and
wounded on both sides. The fight went on in the universities, even in the intermediate schools. Isolated
Jews, suddenly hated, boycotted and attacked by former
comrades, sometimes killed themselves in despair. In
the countrysides, bands of debt-burdened farmers raised
the Black Flag of the Peasant Wars, hurled bombs,
burned houses and hayricks, murdered. The reactionaries were not always the aggressors, but it was
they who turned a peaceful people into a nation of
brutal brawlers. . . . Murder, nationalism and ob-
scurantism stalked boldly through the country. . . .
Youth, habitually impatient and forward-looking, had
turned its back on the present. . . . Idealizing, not a
progressive future, but a romanticized past. . . . Unemployment was the seed-bed of the hatred and chaos
and reaction, but the chief gardener was Adolf Hitler.

HOOVER MORATORIUM

The events which led up to the offer from
President Hoover of a year's Moratorium on
all Inter-Government debts; the London Con-

ference of July 20, 1931, which practically
accepted it; and the financial instability which
forced Britain off the Gold Standard on
September 21, 1931, need not be here detailed.
The outstanding points not to be forgotten are
that the panic which led to the withdrawal of
credits from Germany aggravated the industrial
despair and caused Hindenburg's S O S appeal
to President Hoover. Hoover's proposal of a
one-year Moratorium, suspending all payments
of interest and principle on Inter-Government
debts, was not accepted until France agreed
and the London Conference (July 20) handed
the question over to Central and private
banks and the Bank of International Settle-
ments (at Basel), recommending that credits
to Germany should be renewed. On August 1,
1931, Germany passed out of immediate danger
and normal banking payments were renewed.
The renewed demand for the payment of
short loans in London led to Britain "going off
Gold," September 21, 1931.

DISARMAMENT

·During the years 1930 and 1931 the question
of Disarmament was being discussed in view
of the Disarmament Conference at Geneva to
open in February 1932. President Hoover
repeatedly stated the American view that
European nations were spending on armaments
and warlike preparations what rendered them

too poor to pay their War Debts to U.S.A. The countries of Europe were plainly told that if they would not disarm they must not expect American Creditors to be lenient. At Geneva the German delegates demanded that as Germany was disarmed the promises of the Covenant of the League should be honoured and real disarmament should follow.

THE "ANSCHLUSS"

In March 1931 the desire of Germany and Austria to be united politically (in the *Anschluss*) was revived by the proposal of their Ministers for a complete Customs Union between the two Countries. Made at a time when these Countries wanted loans, credits and *Standstill* agreements, the proposal seemed reasonable to them as knocking down one of the Tariff Walls and being offered for extension to other countries; but from the first it excited strong opposition; the Little Entente Powers held it a violation of Peace Treaties; Briand found it conflicting with his plan of a European Federation. It was dropped for the time, to be revived as one of the objects of Hitler's National policy to unite in one land the whole German race.

CHAPTER VII

REICHSTAG WEAKER. HITLER STRONGER

Conditions of 1931 Favour Hitler—Nazi Increase of Votes—Great Events of 1932—President Hindenburg—Hindenburg Re-elected President—Hindenburg Dismisses Brüning—Lausanne Conference—German Withdrawal from Disarmament Conference—Hitler's Policy—von Schleicher Chancellor—German Claim to Equality in Arms—New Year 1933 Opens Ominously—Hitler Chancellor

CONDITIONS OF 1931 FAVOUR HITLER

THE year 1931, *Annus Terribilis*, meant everywhere less Parliamentary rule and more unusual dictatorial measures to avoid world chaos. Conditions weakened Parliaments, especially the Reichstag. Dictatorships were nearly inevitable. If the world conditions had not suited so well Hitler's aims and claims in 1931, he could not have grasped in 1933 the absolute power.

NAZI INCREASE OF VOTES

.The growth of Nazi Polling forces is shown by these figures of the Party's votes:

May 1924: Reichstag Election, 1,918,310 votes.
May 1928: Reichstag Election, 809,541 votes (setback!)
September 1930: Reichstag Election, 6,406,397 votes (intense and violent campaign, with great money resources and grave unemployment).
April 1932: Second Ballot for President, Hitler chal-

D

lenging the great Hindenburg; Hindenburg, 19,359,642 votes and Hitler, 13,417,460 votes.

These figures show the steady advance of Hitler to power. Barely one year lies between March 13, 1932, and March 5, 1933. In March 1932 Hitler was challenging as a reactionary the re-election of the honoured President of the Republic. In March 1933 President Hindenburg had made him his Chancellor and Hitler had gained a Reichstag vote which made him Dictator of the Third Reich.

GREAT EVENTS OF 1932

To observe the progress of events during 1932 will help to understand the Nazi Triumph which has come in 1933.

PRESIDENT HINDENBURG

Marshal von Hindenburg, President of the Republic, was beloved at home and respected abroad. He was loyal to the Republic, though a monarchist. He used his powers well, tried to get conflicting interests to work together in the Cabinet and in legislation. At his advanced age of 85 he was inclined to retire from office. But being pressed to offer himself for re-election, which was expected to be without opposition, he consented, knowing that no one could combine the same authority, popularity and general support which he enjoyed. That Hitler should have challenged his re-election shocked and surprised many both in Germany and abroad. When in 1932 there were so many millions against the old President it was a warning that was ominous.

March 13, 1932.—First Ballot for Election of President resulted in Hindenburg receiving 18,661,736 votes, Hitler 11,338,571; Hindenburg not receiving majority over the total poll a second ballot was required. The Communist Thälmann polled nearly 5,000,000.
March 17 and 18.—Raids on 107 Nazi offices and quarters by police showed that Nazi Storm detach-

ments (S.A. = Sturm Abtheilungen) had stood
ready to await orders from Hitler at Munich and
plans were prepared for a Putsch.

March 19.—Nazi press announcement that 350,000
S.A. men had been mobilized "to avoid disturbances" on polling day. Hitler was admittedly
ready to go into civil war; he hesitated to do so
with Hindenburg on the other side.

April 1.—Reports that the Nazi Brown Army had
dominated Brunswick, terrorized the population,
attacked unarmed and peaceable citizens, with a
view to the Presidential Second Ballot.

April 2.—The Ex-Crown Prince issued Manifesto to
support Hitler at the poll.

April 5.—Prussian Ministry issued statement with docu-
mentary evidence of the Nazi preparations for their
civil war; Nazi plans to subvert the police, etc.

HINDENBURG RE-ELECTED PRESIDENT

April 10, 1932.—Second Ballot for President resulted
in Hindenburg's Election with 19,359,642 votes.
Hitler had nearly 13,500,000 and the Communist
less than 4,000,000 votes. Hindenburg re-elected
President by nearly 6,000,000 majority.

April 13.—Hindenburg signed a Decree for the safe-
guarding of the State, ordering immediate dissolution of the S.A. bodies of the Nazi Party (but not
of the Nazi Party itself), with their staffs, air-corps,
barracks, etc. The official statement recalled that
in 1929 had been similarly dissolved the "Red
Fighting Front," Communist private army.

April 14.—Hitler answered this decree by a Manifesto
to his "former comrades" (the S.A. men, etc.) saying,
"Our reply to this latest desperate effort of the
'System' will not be a parade but a kick. April 24
is the day of retribution." "The System" is the
Nazi word of contempt for the Weimar Republic;
April 24 was the Polling Day for the State Parlia-
ments of Germany.

April 24.—The State Parliament (Diet, Landtag) Elections resulted in sweeping Nazi gains; the Republican Coalition of Catholics, Democrats and Social-Democrats in Prussia, the defenders of Republican democracy, were in a minority; the reactionaries, of whom the Nazis were the dominant element, could change the whole State order.

April 26.—A Communist Manifesto invited Social-Democrats and other workers' organizations to unite "to defeat capitalist robbers and the even more insolent Fascist bands." The hopeless opposition of Communists to the other Labour parties had only put power into their exploiters' hands.

May 12.—Violent attack by Nazis in the Reichstag led to suspension of sitting and of Nazi members for "gross disorder."

May 24.—Reichstag Foreign Relations Committee adopted resolution demanding Government affirmation of Germany's equal rights to arm and another defying Poland not to attack the rights of Free City of Danzig.

May 30.—The end of Brüning as Chancellor; he had in recent speeches demanded the joint action of the world to overcome "the scourge of unemployment"; "one-fifth of the German population consisted of unemployed and their dependants; no wonder that hundreds of thousands of young men, unable to get work, set their hopes on the destruction of existing conditions." Brüning demanded of President Hindenburg a reassurance of his support and his signature to necessary decrees, one of which was to effect reduction of salaries, pensions and "Dole" payments; he was refused and resigned.

HINDENBURG DISMISSES BRÜNING

It has occasioned wide surprise that Hindenburg should have so treated Brüning with whom he had worked so long and cordially, and should have chosen as

his successor an unknown and unpopular Catholic
Baron. Had he been over-persuaded by the East
Prussian Junkers? He belonged to that caste.

June 4, 1932.—President Hindenburg, on the advice of
his cabinet, dissolved the Reichstag. The Cabinet
of von Papen (Cabinet of Barons) had seven members of the old Nobility class; their electoral declaration accused Brüning of having "weakened the
moral strength of the nation."

June 16.—A decree was issued lifting the ban on the
Brown Army; the wearing of uniforms was resumed
at once by the Nazi S.A., the Stahlhelm and the
Republican Reichsbanner. As a result of this, street
fighting and the numbers of political murders
increased.

June 17.—In Bavaria, where reaction was strong though
Hitler's followers numerically weak, great violence
was shown by the Nazis in the Diet where over
forty Nazis were forcibly expelled.

LAUSANNE CONFERENCE

Von Papen at the Lausanne Conference effected a
conditional settlement of Reparations. The Lausanne Settlement remains unratified; yet in practice
it swept away the prospect that any Reparation
Demand will be made on Germany.

July 1932.—This month recorded an aggravation of
the warfare of the private armies; at Hamburg
12 persons were killed; in one week-end 17 were
killed in various places; Socialist newspapers were
suspended for "statements calculated to bring the
Chancellor into contempt." Von Papen, returning
from Lausanne, where on July 9 the Agreement
was signed ending Reparations, met with strong
opposition from Hitler and Hugenberg.

July 11.—Statement made that the Reichswehr authorities had agreed that Nazi Storm Troops were
to be used for future frontier defence.

July 20.—President Hindenburg signed decrees (1) making the Chancellor von Papen Reich Commissioner for Prussia with power to dismiss the Prussian Ministers and exercise all powers of the Prussian Minister President (Premier), and (2) imposing on Berlin and Brandenburg a "state of emergency" with Articles of the Constitution suspended, personal liberties and rights and freedom of press also suspended, death penalties prescribed for certain offences, and summary courts provided without appeal therefrom. Protests of the Prussian officials met with forcible removal and imprisonment; their appeals on legality of these proceedings went to the Supreme Court at Leipzig, only to be adjudicated when the battle had been lost and won. Thus the police and other powers of the Prussian State were now controlled by the Reich Government; this step in the unification of the German Empire Bismarck and the Kaiser had never dared to make. Here was enacted as a temporary emergency the submerging of a Confederate State's independence and freedom. Hitler was without effort to effect constitutional change by which the German Confederation became a centralized unified State.

July 29.—Hindenburg decreed a political truce, no meetings for ten days.

July 31.—Reichstag Election resulted in the Nazis being the largest party, over 13,700,000 votes and 229 seats, but not a clear majority over the rest. The Election was succeeded by intense violence and street fighting, Nazis the chief aggressors, some Socialists and Communists killed in cold blood; week-end murders 25; 420 arrests in Berlin; attacks on Socialists and Jews reported from many places. At Königsberg police admit the outrages there to be the work of Nazis, of whom 51 arrested confess to acts of incendiarism.

August 13.—Hitler, after discussing with von Papen reconstruction of the Cabinet, has interview with President Hindenburg. Refusing offers of the Vice-Chancellorship, Premiership of Prussia, Ministry of Interior and other offices, Hitler demanded as Leader of the largest party in the Reichstag the Chancellorship and complete power, "the same position as that which Mussolini received after the March on Rome." Hindenburg refused this request because his "duty would not allow him to transfer the whole power of Government exclusively to the National-Socialist Party, which proposed to wield this power one-sidedly." It was officially stated that the President earnestly admonished Hitler to carry on chivalrously.

August 22.—At Beuthen five Nazis who had coldbloodedly murdered a Communist were sentenced to death. Hitler sent a telegram to the convicts saying the verdict is "monstrous"; manifesto issued by Hitler that "your liberty is a question of our honour," and "our duty to fight against the Government," "von Papen has written his name in history with the blood of patriotic Germans." The sentences were, after appeals for mercy by parties opposed to the Nazis, commuted to imprisonment for life. The murderers were finally released by Hitler.

September 7.—Hitler, speaking at Munich, expressed readiness to work with other parties, "he had no ambition for the title of Chancellor. He wanted the leadership of the German Nation. I am convinced that nothing can happen to me, for I know that I have been appointed to my task by Providence."

September 12.—Tense disagreement in the Reichstag between the Nazi Party and the Chancellor von Papen. A vote being taken which would have overthrown the Government, the Chancellor laid on the table a document dissolving the Reichstag. After Göring had questioned the legality of the dissolution, it was admitted that the dissolution held good.

GERMAN WITHDRAWAL FROM DISARMAMENT CONFERENCE

September 30, 1932.—Germany withdrew from the Disarmament Conference at Geneva "until the question of her equality of status has been settled." Eventually the Four Power Conference in London decided in recognition of Germany's claim for equality and Germany returned to join the Conference Discussions.

HITLER'S POLICY

October 20 and 24, 1932.—Hitler in speeches declares the new foreign policy is based on close co-operation with Britain and Italy and not on attempts to reconciliate France, not to make promises not to re-arm, but to fix on France alone the responsibility; whether the German state should be monarchist, that "was Germany's business," "as so much presses, we are glad not to have to deal with the question" now.

November 6.—Reichstag Election resulted in Nazis getting 11,700,000 votes, 196 seats; Social-Democrats 7,200,000 votes, 121 seats; Communists nearly 6,000,000 votes, 100 seats; Centre (Catholics) 4,000,000 votes, 70 seats; Nationalists 3,000,000 votes, 51 seats. Just four months before the Nazis made a dictatorship which abolished virtually all parties save their vassal allies, the Nationalists, they only polled 1 vote in 3 of the whole electorate. This was the last occasion when Germans could exercise any pretence of a free vote for the Reichstag.

November 24.—Hindenburg offers Hitler, as leader of the largest party, the Chancellorship; Hitler declined because he was not offered the full "Presidial" powers; Hindenburg put it thus, "I cannot give to the leader of a party my Presidial powers; such a Cabinet is bound to develop into a party dictatorship and increase the tension among the German people."

VON SCHLEICHER CHANCELLOR

December 2, 1932.—General von Schleicher, whom Hitler had refused to meet, formed a Government as the Chancellor; he retained the Ministry of Defence himself; von Papen was not a member of the Cabinet.

GERMAN CLAIM TO EQUALITY IN ARMS

December 11, 1932.—At Geneva the Five Powers, Britain, France, Italy, Germany and U.S.A. agreed in the Declaration that "one of the principles that should guide the Disarmament Conference should be the grant to Germany . . . of equality of rights" to arm, this to be "embodied in the convention containing the conclusions of the Conference." The declaration reasserted the renunciation of "any attempt to resolve any present or future differences between signatories by resort to force."

December 21.—The Christmas of 1932 seemed to offer some hope of more steady and peaceful progress. Von Schleicher was a declared non-party man, attempted to approach and conciliate Republicans as well as Nationalists, put forward bold plans for improving industry and by a Presidial decree "for the maintenance of internal peace" made an effort to appease violence. Von Papen's decrees, which throttled the press and shut up public meetings, etc., were replaced by milder forms. An Amnesty Law let out of prison 10 to 15,000 political prisoners, mostly Nazis. The numbers attest the extent to which street fighting had been practised.

NEW YEAR 1933 OPENS OMINOUSLY

January 4, 1933.—An ominous opening for the New Year, when Hitler met von Papen for the first time since August 1932. They discussed "bringing the Nazis into a Government of National Concentra-

tion," no question of a removal of the Cabinet of
the day.

January 28.—Chancellor von Schleicher asked Hindenburg for authority to dissolve the Reichstag if a
no-confidence motion was passed; on this being
refused von Schleicher resigned. In doing so he
warned Hindenburg against appointing a Government which would represent only one party.

HITLER CHANCELLOR

January 30, 1933.—Hitler was appointed Chancellor
and formed with the Nationalists a Cabinet, which
contained von Papen as Vice-Chancellor and five
other Nationalists, but Nazis in the key posts.

CHAPTER VIII

HITLER: THE MAN AND HIS METHODS

Adolf Hitler—The Nazi Party—Hitler in the Munich Putsch—Hitler's Book: "My Struggle"—Hitler in Leipzig Court—Hitler's Belief in Himself—Hitler as Orator—Hitler in His Meetings—Hitler and the Masses—Nazi Publications—Nazi Flag and Swastika—Hitler's Authority.

ADOLF HITLER

ADOLF HITLER, an orphan boy of 17 in Vienna, had a few shillings and a roll of drawings in his pocket! He had been refused admission as student to the Art School; he was told that he might try to become an Architect! In 1912 he went on to Munich and still tried to draw and design while earning his living in the building trade. After serving four years in the German Army, 1914–18, he heard the news of the German capitulation; he was a wounded soldier in hospital; he turned to cry into his pillow and swore to restore German glory. Back in 1919 at Munich, with a few others, the romantic soldier started a new political party, himself the seventh member, the German Labour Party. Twelve years later this Adolf Hitler was Chancellor and Dictator of Germany. The orphan boy had become the most successful artist in the world, with his word-pictures of a new Third German Empire, of Aryan Manhood aroused to crush inferior races, a master producer of films, shows, pageants and dramas, in all of which he was himself the leading figure. Genius and brilliantly successful, this man is both an artist and a politician.

He was born in 1889 in Austria, just across the River Inn from Bavaria; his father was a Customs officer. The home was a simple, pious Catholic, German home. When, in 1906, he went to Vienna, he was disgusted and indignant with the gay dissipation and strange Jewish element in the luxurious cosmopolitan city. He accepted the socialistic aims and the anti-semite bitterness of the Christian-Socialist Party. Its leader, the notorious Dr. Lueger, inocculated him with a virus which has remained in the form of a chronic *Judenhetze*. In 1912, aged 23, he moved to Munich, did not give up trying to paint pictures, but had to earn his livelihood as handy man and unskilled labourer in the building trade. He began to argue and orate, a bit of a Socialist already. In 1914, though still an Austrian citizen, he was accepted as a volunteer in the German Army, served till the end of the Great War on the Western Front, was twice wounded, reached the rank of corporal, was awarded the Iron Cross. Back in Munich in 1919 he was in the period of turbulence when Kurt Eisner was in power supported by the proletarian uprising; when

Eisner was murdered and a Reactionary and intensely Bavarian Government ruled, the French schemed to detach Bavaria from Prussia, pursuing the *separatist* policy which later was attempted and failed in Western Germany. Hitler, possessed of his duty of making the German Nation a united power, had a vision that Germany until united could not be at peace at home nor powerful abroad. He was loud in his spoutings with his new political party, the German Labour Party; he was entered as "No. 7" on his card.

THE NAZI PARTY

The Party was merged in Streicher's German Socialist Party of Nuremberg, a larger political organization, which became the National-Socialist German Labour Party (NSDAP = the Nazis, name derived thus: *NAt*ional-so*Z*Ialist). In this band was a young engineer, Gottfried Feder, a clever fellow with smart superficiality, whose future eminence was bound up with the ideas of his theory of Interest-Thraldom (Zinsenknechtschaft) which he instilled into the · receptive Hitler.

HITLER IN THE MUNICH PUTSCH

The first appearance made by Hitler of a prominent public nature was when he took part in the abortive Munich Putsch made by Ludendorff in November 1923. It was a melodramatic affair; in the big Beer Cellar (Bürger-Brau-Keller) he fired his pistol into the ceiling, threatened at the pistol's point the frightened Premier von Kahr to give his unwilling adhesion. Hitler put his name at the foot of a placard announcing the New *German National Government*; the other names were those of General Ludendorff and two high officers. When Reichswehr guards cleared the streets with rifles, several young hot-heads were shot dead. Hitler saved himself by a fall which broke his collar-bone on the stones. The victims have been immortalized as heroes who died to found the Third Empire. Hitler was condemned by a Court, which gave no verdict in the case of Ludendorff, but sentenced Hitler to five years' imprisonment.

HITLER'S BOOK: "MY STRUGGLE"

Before eight months of the sentence were passed, Hitler was released. He had enjoyed it with easy conditions and what he needed—a calm period to clear his mind, make his plans and write his life. *My Struggle* (Mein Kampf) was the result. The book is frank and lengthy, conceited, so full of self-confidence and intolerant opinions. It has been a "best-seller," and passed (with very few emendations) into fourteen large editions. It has added thousands of marks to his Party funds and thousands to the Party membership. The average British citizen would be surprised at its advocacy of terrorism as a party policy and its welcome to the prospect of a *Judenhetze*.

HITLER IN LEIPZIG COURT

The skill and audacity of Hitler are abundantly evidenced in his actions; they can always be related by himself in his speeches and by his press, so as to prove him a great Leader. Take his appearance before the Court at Leipzig as a witness in 1930; certain officers of the Reichswehr were charged with forming Nazi "Cells" in the Army. They called Hitler to prove that the Nazi policy was loyal and peaceful. Hitler swore that "We shall attain our goal by legal means" (*auf legalem Weg*). These were words to satisfy and attract the steady old folk. In the next breath, asked "what about the men whom you say were the arch-traitors of November 9, 1918 (those who made the Armistice)? how about them if your party attains power?" Hitler replied, "Then heads will roll" (*Dann werden Köpfe rollen*). Both these replies have passed into Nazi slogans. Hitler would probably say, without any conscious self-deception, that the arch-traitors of 1918 set up a "System" which is so *illegal* that it will be quite legal to execute them without further question.

HITLER'S BELIEF IN HIMSELF

The career and success of Hitler are unparalleled. Hitler has intense faith in his cause, in himself as Divinely appointed to achieve its victory, in the "pure Aryan" race and the German Nation. He has shown restless energy and resource in himself and has inspired these qualities in thousands whose devotion to "The Leader" is a religion and a delight. He uses savagery in word and deed against his fellow-countrymen, if they oppose him; he has carried these to such limits that what would appear as Brutality, not to say Barbarity, in Britain are praised as firmness and just retaliation in Germany.

To these qualifications for playing a great part in the political life of mankind he cannot bring the refinement and distinction of birth, breeding or education, nor of a fine physique, handsome presence or noble physiognomy. In their place he has simple unaffected manners, a friendly cameraderie and charm, ease and accessibility, cheerful confidence and earnest concentration passing from him to his followers.

Adolf Hitler remained an Austrian subject till on February 26, 1932, he took the oath of loyalty to the German State; Germany being then a Republic under the Weimar Constitution, which Hitler was out to destroy. The opening to become German and to take his seat in the Reichstag, in which the then largest party acknowledged his leadership, was conveniently provided for him by the State of Brunswick, which had already a Nazi Government in office.. Brunswick appointed him a minor official; his office carried with it the duty to become a German citizen with the usual formalities. In U.S.A. the President must be an American from birth. The acquisition of British citizenship has strict conditions. In Germany, denied real unity with Austria by foreign domination, an Austrian, speaking German and suffering from the Peace Treaties, has for years been regarded as a fellow-citizen by Germans.

HITLER AS ORATOR

These characteristics explain why Hitler is a magnificent orator, not for the forensic or deliberate assembly, but as an agitator and popular demagogue. His style and manner suit the traditions and temperament of the German people so exactly that he is more unapproachable as the spokesman of the hour than ever John Bright in the nineteenth, or Lloyd George in the twentieth, centuries. The skill, tact, subtlety and simplicity of his speeches, often of great length and of little intellectual or political contents, mostly a simple theme with endless variations, would perplex and bore a philosopher. They were never intended to argue with thinkers. They were made to gain the masses.

HITLER IN HIS MEETINGS

Hitler has used every modern means and scientific invention to enhance the attraction, and deepen the impression, of his meetings.

E

People want shows, amusement, novelties, and emotional stimulus and are ready to pay for these everywhere. Advent of Hitler at a Monster meeting! Arrival from a distance by aeroplane! Fleet of many aircraft, etc.! Huge halls, seats booked and paid for weeks beforehand, elaborate decoration with flags, mottoes, emblems and symbols, order kept by the uniformed and well-drilled Brown Shirts, and the S.S. black-shirted élite of Hitler's Private Army, the Defence Squads (S.S. = Schutz-Staffel); and, of course, music, bands and community singing of National (Hitlerite) hymns of hate against the Jews and Te Deums of HEIL! Hitler! Then the formal entry of Hitler himself, in solemn almost religious procession, whereat the Assembly rise to a man, hold forth right hands in Roman Fascist Salute. At length the Leader speaks, not to argue or to convince, but to denounce the Versailles Treaty, to command his followers in the name of the Nation and to promise to every class and individual things beyond their expectation. Such were the mass meetings in hundreds of German cities in the two years leading up to the sensational Reichstag Poll of September 1930, when the Nazis polled nearly six-and-a-half million votes.

HITLER AND THE MASSES

Hitler owed this astounding oratorical ascendency to various means, which he used with cleverness and insight. The Capitalists and Reactionaries, the big firms, cartels, combines and manufacturers, both in Germany and in lands outside, had been giving for years from 1918 onwards millions of marks to the reactionary parties and organizations to combat Bolshevism and Communism; Hitler's abuse of the Social-Democrats and Communists was strong enough for him to obtain large subventions from the Capitalists, though his party began, and still stands, as a *Labour* Party and has always insisted, as it does to-day, that Nazis are Socialists. Hitler has always had ample funds, not only from Reactionaries of many kinds and Nations, but from the voluntary subscriptions of his party members, from the tickets sold for, and collections at, his meetings. It added to Hitler's fame that his meetings could be relied on to be orderly and enthusiastic. His Private Army, the Brown Shirts, took care of that. They had instructions how to create uproar at the meetings of other parties, but they were in force and under control so that Hitler's speeches were uninterrupted and the response well led and unanimous. The steady, quiet-loving and elderly citizens, with no party ties, at first hesitated, but soon crowded in to join what was essentially a movement of young men who had not been in the War. Imitating Hitler's propaganda methods, after his enormous party vote in September 1930, the other parties took leaves out of the Nazi book; they were late in the field and they could not rely on the rich men's money-chests. The Reichsbanner, the Private Army of the Social-Democrats, became a very big concern, with attractions, sports-grounds, swimming-baths and drilling-grounds, which were also part of Hitler's planning.

NAZI PUBLICATIONS

The Nazis have their special Publishing Firm (Eher-Verlag, Munich). Its Full List of Publications contains speeches, pamphlets, and topical, electoral and other works, with no names of authority or standing outside the well-known figures of the Hitler ranks. There are

Nazi Pamphlets, edited by Gottfried Feder, 44 mono-
graphs on various events and subjects, in a style agree-
able to the Nazi temperament. Picture books and gift
books in "elegant bindings" offer choice for young and
old. There are Feder's explanations and notes to the
"unalterable" Party Programmes of which there is an
English Translation at one Mark. (Further account of
the Programme will be found in the following chapter,
see pp. 131 ff.).

Hitler's genius is seen in so many directions that one
cannot reasonably say that he is a fanatic and a patriotic
wind-bag with no prospect to remain at the head after
he has obtained Full Power. His fanaticism is narrow,
National, defiant of other nations and races, but he has
Vision and like all great actors in the world's drama
he can "suit the action to the word and the word to
the action." He knows what, whom and when to drop
or retain. This applies to his slogans, symbols, mascots,
signs and "Parole" (Watch-words). No need for Hitler
to offer prizes in Slogan Competitions! he invents them
himself, "Germany awake!" "Towards the Third
Empire" recalled his eloquent periods about "The First
Holy Roman Empire," destroyed by the discords of the
various States, and "The Second Empire" (Bismarck
and Kaiser) destroyed by the treachery of the "Marxists"
and sold by the Jews in Germany, these now to be
redeemed by the "Third Empire," won by the Nazis,
led by himself. Thus would be saved for ever the great
pure German-blood Nation; the Jews would be "exterminated"; it would be done by himself. Here came
in another slogan, "Death to the Jews."

NAZI FLAG AND SWASTIKA

The Hitler Flag, with its Black Swastika, was
adopted by the party in its first Party Congress
in Munich in 1921. A Nazi publication says of
this event that "the banners puzzled the people
who did not understand the meaning of these

emblems. We sum up in the Flag our Programme: Red marks the social character, the white the national features, and the hooked cross the Aryan mission of our movement." (Translation as given in *Bilddokumente der Zeit: Hitler*, p. 30, Berlin, 1932.) So it is clear that Persecution of the Jews (*Judenhetze*) is the central sign of the Nazi Flag, the Swastika. The Swastika, the four equal-arm hooked cross, one of the most ancient mystic symbols, found widely distributed over the world, was adopted as the Aryan symbol, and anti-Jewish. At the Kapp Putsch the rebels wore it and it is now the universal badge of Hitler's army and party. As the Fasces is now the Italian sign equal in honour and significance to the Italian National Flag, so the Nazi Flag, which bears the Swastika, is to be flown everywhere with the old Black-white-red tricolour flag of the Second German Empire. The Weimar Republican Flag, Black-red-gold, has been declared illegal. To display it became a crime in Germany. The Nazi Flag is a red ground and large white disc, charged with Swastika in black. The cult and development of Nazi Flag, Swastika and Slogan have not been neglected by Hitler, who knows the love of mascots and symbols by the superstitious and politically immature.

HITLER'S AUTHORITY

Hitler knew how men and women find the claims of authority hard to resist and the relief that most women and many men feel in being told by someone claiming authority or infallibility what to believe. If a strong personality insists that any doctrine is certain, he can get someone to trust him; if he is absolutely sincere and devoted to this doctrine, he is sure of devoted followers. Hitler has assumed the power to make the programme of the party and the party has declared it to be unalterable.

Party Conferences in democratic lands discuss their politics, varying the order and urgency of the party programme's items; how straightforward and simple it is to have an oracular voice to say once for all what the true gospel is! Pious Islam believes the Koran to be literally inspired. American fundamentalists believe this of the Bible. Nazis include in their slogan "All power to Hitler." Hitler's word is verbally inspired in the Nazi Programme! His Will shall be done in the Enabling Act (Ermächtigungs-Gesetz)!

CHAPTER IX

NAZIS AND NATIONALISTS

*Hitler's Cabinet—Von Papen—Von Neurath—Hugen-
berg — Seldte — Schacht — Von Blomberg— Von
Krosigk—Gürtner—Rübenaich—Nationalist Ministers
but Nazi Policy—Göring—Goebbels—Frick—Kerrl—
Rosenberg—Rosenberg's Mission to London—Feder
—Röhm—The Nazi Prospect*

HITLER'S CABINET

HITLER became Dictator of Germany when
Hindenburg appointed him Chancellor. He
had von Papen, Hindenburg's special friend,
as Vice-Chancellor, to give the Nationalists
their proper weight. Hindenburg expected that
his appeal to Hitler to act "chivalrously"
would be fairly responded to. Besides, there
were to be in the Cabinet half a dozen non-
Nazi members; these included von Neurath as
Foreign Minister, and the leader of the
Nationalist Party, Alfred Hugenberg. The
prospects seemed to point to a firmly established
Government and an end to the unceasing
Elections, with their street fighting and dis-
turbance to trade, and to general confidence.
He could expect no General Election for four
years, no repeated Cabinet crisis, changes of
Governments, and easy complacency in his
task of signing emergency decrees. If Hinden-

burg so expected, it is not what has occurred. The Government has been Nazi in spirit and deed, though in Cabinet and profession it has been Nazi-Nationalist. It will be well to examine the leading figures in the new system of Hitler's dictatorship, which has come to destroy *The System* Republic. Here is a *Who's Who* of Hitler's Cabinet.

VON PAPEN

Von Papen was military attaché in Washington till sent away by U.S.A. for German activities which suggest that this pious Catholic, from an old Westphalian house, a former cavalry officer, in the most select Junker circles, is of pliant moral principles. He belonged to the Catholic party (Centre) and owned the Catholic newspaper *Germania*; he was a surprise when appointed by Hindenburg as Chancellor of his Cabinet of Barons on Brüning's dismissal. Von Papen acted as German representative at the Lausanne Conference, where his excellent French and refined manners helped to reach the agreement and the conditional promise of a German payment. On his return to Berlin he was bitterly attacked for his action by Hitler and Hugenberg. Though in February Minister of the Interior for Prussia, he was removed from that position that Göring might be placed where he could direct the Terror and campaign against Marxists and Jews.

VON NEURATH

Von Neurath, the new Minister for Foreign Affairs, is an experienced diplomatist; he has been correct and successful under the Republican "System" since the War, in Copenhagen, in Rome from 1922 to 1930; his nearness to Mussolini there and knowledge

of Fascism in Italy is a good point; so is his term
of office as Ambassador in London from 1930 to
1933. He must know what is thought of the
Judenhetze in Rome and England. If Germany's
Foreign Policy (as Hitler promises) is in close co-
operation with Italy and Britain, no better appointment could have been made.

HUGENBERG

Alfred Hugenberg, born in Hanover in 1865, has been
described by Mowrer as "pre-eminent among the
dispensers of Hatred, an able stern strong-willed
and uncongenial personality." The Nazi book about
Nazi leaders accepts what was often said of him,
"Kein Mensch—eine Mauer" (Not a man—a wall).
He was the most outstanding reactionary till Hitler
rose; he had amassed great wealth, had given
liberally to Hitler's funds as well as to the Stahlhelm, the private army of the Nationalists; he is
a press magnate, controls 150 papers, and owns the
Telegraph Agency which supplies the local papers
in Germany; his influence exceeds in opportunities
for press power what Hearst in U.S.A. or Lord
Rothermere exerts in England. He owns, and takes
care to use for advancing reactionary views, the
U.F.A. (Universal Film Assn.), the Company which
produces the Movies and owns numerous theatres.
He is an agricultural expert and has the office of
Minister of Agriculture and Economic Affairs.

SELDTE

Franz Seldte, Minister of Labour in Hitler's Cabinet;
a fierce, humorous, rough and restless soldier, so
full of fight and relentless hatred of the men who
had made the Armistice that on Christmas Day
1918 he got together *Frontkameraden* in Madgeburg
and the Stahlhelm was founded. Both the oldest
and most respectable of the private armies, it has
played a great part in Germany ever since. Frankly

Monarchist and with the avowed aim of restoring the Military Power (Wehrhaftmachung), mostly composed of the older soldiers and middle-aged patriots, it had Hindenburg for years as President, and numbered half a million. They helped the Brown Shirts at the Elections when all Republican forces were suppressed. It was officially stated in March that "The Stahlhelm now stands firmer than ever. It has overcome opponents and strong official opposition." But a few weeks later Seldte was made to give up his command of the Stahlhelm and to call on them to merge their old order with the Nazi S.A. The serious differences between Stahlhelm and S.A. men in several places led to the Stahlhelm being brought under Hitler's direct dictatorship.

SCHACHT

Hjalmar Schacht, born in 1877 in the Danish district north of Flensburg, of a commercial stock, has a lifelong banking experience; from the beginning of a modest stool in a private bank his abilities took him into the Empire Finance Ministry in 1923; he rose to be Director of the Reichsbank, where his grasp and power of prompt, firm decision made him the strong man; he negotiated the Young Plan, but resigned in March 1930 as a protest against the Government's weakness in face of the Allies. Politically Schacht was "young Liberal," later Democrat, and then Nationalist; never a prominent party man, but passing gradually to the reactionary side. A sound financier, he can insist and get his way; in view of a possible demand for a moratorium for payment due under the Dawes and Young Loans, and with the World Economic Conference ahead, he will play a large part. He is not in the Cabinet, but in a position of great importance; personally "National," but not "Socialist." In April Schacht was sent to Washington for Preliminary talk with Roosevelt in preparation for the

World Economic Conference; he can speak with authority of the grave economic condition of Germany. Should Hitler fail in the reconstruction plans he has foreshadowed, Schacht might be the strong man of sounder financial methods to restore his country, provided the Economic Conference of June 1933 lead to international co-operation and World Recovery. He may be a great figure in the near future. He may even have to ask for a moratorium for payments due on the Dawes and Young Loans. Von Papen, Hugenberg, Seldte and Schacht are the leading Nationalists brought by Hitler into his Government; the other non-Nazis, representatives of the Nationalist party, are reactionaries, notorious for animosity (more or less open in official posts) to the Republic and with qualifications of age and administrative experience.

VON BLOMBERG

General Blomberg, among Nazis as "Not a politician, just a soldier," is Hitler's Reichswehr Minister, Minister of Defence; served long years under the Republic, sworn to defend the Weimar State, both in District commands and Headquarters; was one of German experts at Geneva at the Disarmament Conference when recalled to his Cabinet post; has repeatedly declared that the Wehrmacht (military power) should be above party.

VON KROSIGK

Erich von Krosigk, born 1887, of aristocratic family, from 1920 in the Finance Ministry of the Republic; years of quiet competent service there prepared him to be Finance Minister in von Papen's Cabinet of Barons; he held a Cecil Rhodes Scholarship at Oxford, where in 1907 he took his degree in honours; in England he would be a gentleman; in Germany he supports Hitler as a Nationalist.

GÜRTNER

Franz Gürtner, born 1881, son of a railway official, a genial Bavarian Plebeian, gives a fresh taste to the mixed salad of Hitler's Cabinet: the Reichs Minister of Justice.

RÜBENAICH

Von Eltz-Rübenaich, Postmaster-General, born 1875; distinguished career in Engineering College, held high position in administration of the National Railways; greeted by Nazis as "an *intéressant* union of Nobleman and Official"; not previously known as a politician.

NATIONALIST MINISTERS BUT NAZI POLICY

The seats in the Hitler Cabinet went in generous proportion to the Nationalists; at the March 1933 Election the Nazis had more than three times as many votes as the Nationalists; the Cabinet appointed six weeks previously had more Nationalist Ministers than Nazis. The Nazis won on the slogan "All power to Hitler." Besides, this is the "uprising of the German Youth"; the Nationalist Ministers are elderly men, while Nazi Ministers are younger. The Dictatorship of Hitler must be expected to continue for years; the Reichstag has met to vote itself out of power for the natural term of its life (four years by the Weimar Constitution); it has passed the Enabling Act, by which Hitler can decree what laws and regulations he wishes. Hitler has already silenced any criticism in press, print, private speech or letter, and information of what is said or reported abroad. Of public or international opinion he is defiant. His power over a great nation, which geographically, commercially and industrially exceeds the position of either Italy or Russia, is greater than that exercised by Mussolini in Italy or Stalin

in Russia. Hitler's policy will be administered
through his colleagues. Chief of these are Göring
and Goebbels, while three others, Frick, Rosenberg and Feder, can be included among the men
in power in Germany to-day. Several of these have
both by word and action shown a strong diversion
from the line taken by Hitler; outward unity has
been wonderfully maintained in the Nazi movement. Yet there are signs of divergence, e.g. as
between Hitler and Göring in The Terror, when
Hitler counselled restraint and Göring urged
"barbarity."

GÖRING

Hermann Göring, born 1893, was a famous airman in
the War, succeeding to the position of the German
"Ace," Richthofen, who was shot down behind the
British lines after his record had been reached of
eighty-one enemy aircraft shot down. The British
airmen paid chivalrous honour to Richthofen's
grave; chivalry is not to be expected from the most
coarse and savage Jew-baiter Göring: "the Third
Empire will treat Jews like plant lice." He was the
first Nazi to be elected Reichstag President; became
responsible for the Police control in Prussia early
in the Hitler dictatorship, von Papen and his more
respectable methods giving place to the full-blooded
Hitlerite; Göring's mission to Rome in April 1933,
when von Papen also visited the Pope and both
were received by Mussolini, was ominous. Göring
and Goebbels are the two Nazi Ministers most in
the Nazi picture. Both are, like Hitler, Roman
Catholics.

GOEBBELS

Joseph Goebbels was born in 1897, of Westphalian
peasant parents; studied at eight Universities; a
Doctor of Philosophy (with distinctions); joined
the Nazi Party in 1922; always a violent revolutionary and Socialist; his eloquence, youth, intensity

and extreme opinions assured him with Göring a most important position in the Nazi ranks; for his high intelligence and intensity as editor of *Attack* (Angriff) and as Press, Propaganda and Publicity Minister Hitler owes him much; his description of Prussia shows how he unites Prussian reaction with Socialism: "breeding, order, service to society, iron discipline, unconditional authority, political leadership, a strong army, a solid, incorruptible bureaucracy, national prosperity produced by the tenacious energy of its inhabitants and the iron thrift of its princes, popular Christian and patriotic education, and beside the individual's attachment to law a generosity of spirit, a liberalism of opinion, a religious tolerance found nowhere else—that is Prussia" (much of this is, of course, mythical or insincere; but Goebbels is a prince of advertisers). Goebbels is the Election Director and Agent *par excellence*; in every respect Hitler's right-hand man.

FRICK

Wilhelm Frick, born in 1877, studied law and took his degree "Doctor Juris," which pointed his way to a legal career; from 1923 he was noted for his bold efforts in Hitler's fighting gang, sentenced in 1924 for High Treason to 15 months' imprisonment; in closest friendship with Hitler, elected to the Reichstag; in 1930 he became Cabinet Minister in Thuringia; his audacity, energy and clear sense of what he could do made his administrative acts a surprising forecast of what Hitlerism was going to do. Mowrer (pp. 205–6) says that "he began by increasing his own salary, furthered patriotism and religion in the schools . . . introduced into the schools prayers which excited the children against the Revolution and in favour of a war of liberation . . . published edicts against jazz music and modern dancing . . . recommended war literature, books . . . written to encourage the dream about the 'unbeaten army

stabbed in the back' . . . destroyed mural paintings
in Weimar Castle . . . and eliminated from the
galleries fine works as having nothing in common
with 'Nordic German nature' . . . to promote racial
science he made Hans Günther a Professor at Jena
(against the faculty's objection) . . . censored films
and plays; prohibited the political meetings of
opponents, loaned the State Theatre for his own
party's use. In the great building (at Weimar),
where in 1919 the Republican Constitution was
shaped, the Republicans were called a 'Horde of
traitors and cowards.' " Some of these acts were
declared illegal, and Frick's Ministry was ended
by a Ministerial crisis; he had given a sample of
the Nazi idea of pure-German race Culture. His
influence was strongly for Hitler's decision to stand
as Presidential Candidate against Hindenburg unless the latter would dismiss Brüning, who was then
the Chancellor; also resourceful in Hitler's work
of the "unification of Germany," when it was forced
through against the strong State efforts which for
generations had distrusted Prussian domination.
Frick has the key post of Reichs Minister of the
Interior.

KERRL

Hans Kerrl, Minister of Justice, born 1887; fought in
the War; from 1928 a member of the Prussian
Landtag and prominent Nazi; elected Landtag
President in April 1932; placed in control as a
Commissioner in Prussia by von Papen, is also a
member of the Cabinet.

ROSENBERG

Alfred Rosenberg, of Baltic race from Reval, studied
in Moscow, took doctorate in Reval, became a
German citizen in 1923, was in the abortive Hitler
Putsch in 1923; he inspired Hitler with the aim of
German's "Eastern Expansion" as the basis of Nazi
policy; Rosenberg is head of the "Foreign Policy

Department" (set up in April 1933). Rosenberg is the most voluminous of the Nazi writers, for years Editor of the *Völkischer Beobachter*, and an author of books against Judaism, Freemasonry, the Roman Catholic Church; and in favour of Nordic Race theories, and "racial eugenics" and on Foreign Affairs. He has added to Hitler's earlier hatred of the Jews a sublime faith that the highest culture and world future belong to the pure-blooded Aryans, that is, to the German nation; this idea became a weird religious dogma in the Hitler cult; Rosenberg calls it "the belief embodied in the sublime knowledge that Nordic blood represents that Mystery which has replaced and vanquished the ancient sacraments" (Mowrer, p. 291). Rosenberg has made practical suggestions for "racial eugenics"; for keeping the race up to the purest pitch, a risky unsavoury subject, which has not been entirely kept in the background; Hitler himself said on August 7, 1929: "If Germany were to eliminate the weakest 700,000 or 800,000 children of the million born annually, the result would be an increase of National Strength." Rosenberg speaks with authority on Foreign policy, as head of the Foreign Information Department.

ROSENBERG'S MISSION TO LONDON

In May 1933 Rosenberg visited London as the special personal representative of Hitler, requesting through the German Embassy that he might call at the Foreign Office and interview important people. The record and personality of Rosenberg, duly given by the London press, his ignorance of the English language and national character and his appearance and doings in the Metropolis ensured him a press notoriety, many signs of strong disapproval and questions asked in Parliament. All this must have convinced Hitler that the mission was a failure, though it provided illumination on British opinion about the Nazi movement.

FEDER

Gottfried Feder must be recalled here, as one of Hitler's closest friends and spiritual fathers. This young engineer supplied to Hitler what he wanted in his doctrine of Interest-Thraldom, and has elaborated it in his various writings; he has edited the official and "unalterable" "Programme of the Party of Hitler." From this it appears that Hitler wants to eliminate all War-profits and nationalize all Banks and abolish all interest on loans, all property not won by work and the abolition of all profits not made by honest work; and then to all this are added what the Programme promises, great development of Old Age Pensions, lowering of prices and re-valuation of the mark, profit-sharing for all. This fanciful National-Socialism is repugnant to the Nationalist Party Allies of Hitler, but has attracted so many to become Nazi and so cannot now be dropped. Some economists think that Hitler's economic home policy must bring his movement to the ground.

RÖHM

Ernst Röhm, one of the many restless German officers who after 1918 were ready to conspire against the Republic, engage in risky or criminal ventures or go abroad as mercenaries or military instructors, has served in Bolivia as army instructor; he returned to use his organizing experience for building up Hitler's Private Army into the Brown Shirts. As military inspirer he has the ear of The Leader.

THE NAZI PROSPECT

The Cabinet of Hitler combines men of widely different experiences and aims, but united in their determination to rule without Parlia-

F

ment and to destroy the Republic and Constitution of Weimar; in this they have succeeded already. They have established a military non-democratic and non-Parliamentary State, and have "knocked out" the supporters of democracy and pacifism. The Nationalists want the Third Reich to be a restored Monarchy; the Nazis want it to be a Fascist State without an hereditary monarch; in this the Nazis seem the more likely to gain their end. Hitler's home policy favours a Strong State Control and increasing Government interference, restrictions and nationalizing private undertakings in all directions, State monopolies and combinations, with foreign trade brought into agreement. The prospect seems to be that in the struggle between their conflicting aims the force and authority of Hitler will prevail over the older reactionary monarchist policy, and that Germany's future will tend to be that of a National-Socialist Fascist regime.

CHAPTER X

THE REICHSTAG ELECTION OF
MARCH 5, 1933. ITS IMMEDIATE RESULTS

The Election Campaign—Hitler's Utterances—
Threatening Rumours—Communism not the Danger
—The Reichstag Fire—Result of Election of March 5
—Mystery and Suspicions About the Fire

THE ELECTION CAMPAIGN

EVENTS in Germany after Hitler became Chancellor on January 30, 1933, are well known. Episodes like the Reichstag Fire and the responsibility of the Brown Shirts for raids, riots and robbery may not be quite clear. But the main facts are certain. The Private Armies of Hitler and Stahlhelm were active and organized to work with the Police and the Reichswehr, were supplied with fire-arms, were the only forces permitted to demonstrate; they helped Hitler; they obstructed his political opponents. The press of Germany was not as completely subjected to Hitler as it was a month later; but suppressions, for publishing Social-Democrat policy, for mild criticism of the Nazis and often for no reason given, were constant and increasingly severe. Public meetings were attended by the police with Nazi Brown Shirts to keep order. Riots were provoked by the S.A. forces and blood was shed;

from January 1 to February 13 sixty lives
were lost.

Civil War, carried on by the Government's
armed men against unarmed opponents, was
excused by the lurid accounts in the Government press of Communists with secret stores
of arms, their plans for a general massacre,
for wholesale burnings of dwellings, and for
poisoning supplies of food. Believing such
reports, many were ready to accept Hitler's
dictum "there can be no other Germany but
National-Socialism or brutal Communism."
If so, then Communism was the enemy and
everyone against the Government of Hitler
was, if not a Communist, an ally of brutal
Communism; all such were Marxists and
traitors.

HITLER'S UTTERANCES

Hitler had proclaimed for years that he
wanted power to destroy utterly the Republic
and the Marxists. He was equally open in his
campaign speeches; "the only alternative to
Nazi regime was brutal Communism"; "if
he failed of a majority, he would rule without
one; *he* did not make the constitution"; "his
accession to power was not a change of
Government but a change of regime."

Decrees of suppression were accompanied
by dismissals from office, in Prussia especially,
of leading officials; heavy penalties (even

death) for vague offences, e.g. false press reports, or words calculated to discredit the Government, were authorized, to be freely used in Summary Courts from which no appeal was allowed, and in which judges, witnesses and prosecutors were Nazi partisans.

THREATENING RUMOURS

In the week before polling-day rumours were spread that some sudden outburst of increased violence would be seen. . . . From which side? The opponents of Hitler have reason to declare that an intensification of suppression was intended, even to include the actual murder of many, and the immediate violent crushing of the remaining Republican politicians was actually prepared. This course was in fact pursued from February 28. That Hitler and his inner circle were ready for a St. Bartholomew's Night against Marxists, Jews and Pacificists is not inconceivable. The violence of their threats, their admitted "being as good as their word," incitements to bloody deeds in their speeches, in the Nazi songs, in the broadcasts and hints that plots against Hitler's life were likely and discoveries made, with suggestions for what would follow any such attempt—all this produced intense apprehensions of panic and terror.

COMMUNISM NOT THE DANGER

Here let it be emphatically said that Communism was not the real and immediate danger which it has been for years, as a grave threat to the State, Nazis and Nationalists have constantly declared. Lord D'Abernon writes that it was not in his time. The desperately impoverished unemployed thousands swelled the Communist polls; but in personnel and leadership they were weak. Von Papen himself and Conservative papers like the *Kreuz Zeitung* and *Rundschau* and *The Times* contended that there were few organized Communists in the Russian sense, and that the bulk of the German Communists were more or less harmless people who would join any party in desperation.

THE REICHSTAG FIRE

The public atmosphere was exactly attuned to the sensation of the burning of the Reichstag Building on the night of Monday, February 27. The official statement is that the fire was started by a young Dutch Communist, whose confession showed that the Social-Democrats as well as the Communists were parties to the crime. An inquiry has not yet issued any report; no trial of the prisoner accused has taken place. In Germany persons have been severely punished for questioning the truth of

this official statement. The immediate result
of the conflagration was just what Hitler and
his friends desired—an opportunity and excuse
to imprison or completely silence their opponents, branding them as criminals without
any chance of defence or reply. No electioneer-
ing master-stroke ever succeeded so triumph-
antly; for within six hours, at 2 a.m. on
Tuesday, February 28, an Edict was in print
and issued "for the protection of the Reich
from the Communist danger." All Constitutional Articles assuring rights and liberties
were withdrawn; the whole Reich was placed
in a state of emergency; Brown Shirts and
Stahlhelm were to help the police to carry
out all needed measures. A report was soon
produced by Göring "proving beyond a doubt
that leaders of the Communist Party" were
guilty of this atrocity. An alleged statement by
the Dutch Communist was sufficient to include
all the Social-Democrat Party among the
criminals. All Communist Deputies were
arrested, many Socialists saved themselves by
flight or hiding; their whereabouts unknown,
any public utterances from them were of course
impossible. The excitement, rumours, Government monopoly of broadcasting, press and
police, with the Polling Day only four days
ahead, left the Election apparently a "walk-
over" for Hitler and his friends. When Sunday,
March 5, arrived Berlin, all Germany, had a

quiet Election Day. The numbers polling were
a record, over four million more than in
November 1932. There was no need for any
intimidation or coercion at the polls; peaceable
citizens had ground for saying that the city
was in order and saw no street violence. The
completeness of the preparations and the
really wonderful staff-work of the Nazis had
made the desired effect.

The voting was free and the results as
counted and declared are accepted by all as
correct, though suspicion is strong that the
roving Brown Shirts were enabled to vote
more than once.

RESULT OF ELECTION OF MARCH 5

The Election showed that while the opposition
Republican Parties stood firm against Hitler
his Nazis had greatly increased, the Communists having lost over one million supporters;
Hitler had gained five and a half millions
largely in Bavaria and the South, where he
was previously weak. His Nationalist Allies
were weak in votes and had been following
rather than leading in the measures taken.
The panic following on the fire was calmed by
the comparative quiet of the Election Day and
the prospect of the Government Coalition
(Nazis with Nationalists) having a majority
of votes in the new Reichstag. It looked like
better times. This indeed is what numbers of

the German people said. Quiet in the streets,
all the newspapers agreeing that the whole
nation is united and satisfied! At last there is a
Leader who knows his mind, has stated his
policy, and has already received from the
Reichstag power ahead for four years to carry
out his Four-Year Plan! The military power
of the nation acknowledged and soon to be
re-established! not threatening peace but giving
security on German Frontiers!

The average steady middle-class person, not
a politician or party man, may add that the
great Hindenburg was at first against Hitler,
but now is all in his favour, that the Catholic
Church was a short time before declaring that
a good Catholic could not be a Nazi, but now
the Catholic Bishops had withdrawn this ban.
Of course, as to the stories of terrorism and
Jew-baiting, the middle-class family father or
mother says that they have seen nothing of it,
that they know many old officials and leading
Socialist politicians have been eliminated and
some taken into "protective arrest" (Schutzhaft), but that was to keep them safe from
popular indignation or because they have been
guilty of malversation of public moneys or to
prevent their plotting. No "outrages" could
possibly have occurred, not even against the
Jews who have been disloyal to the German
nation, and have abused the liberties enjoyed
in free Germany. All the so-called "terrorism

and outrages" are the lies of foreign journals and Jews. No wonder that people trust and admire Hitler and the Nazis more than ever. Such is the simple faith and devoted patriotism of millions of Germans to-day. Disregarding three things: the votes given at the last Election; the absolute suppression of all German newspapers of any criticism of the Government, of the Nazi actions and of any independent news and facts; and the stern determination of Hitler to rule with his dictatorial power and by reckless terrorism and violent changes, and firmly to found the promised Nationalist-Socialist regime.

To judge the electoral triumph of Hitler properly and to know the real prospects and position of Germany as onlookers abroad see and judge them is not possible to the German people to-day. It is the privilege and duty of friends of Germany and of humanity to study what is under the surface of subdued Germany, not yet at the end of her Revolution and only at the opening of her Fascist regime.

MYSTERY AND SUSPICIONS ABOUT THE FIRE

Notes are here added to give some of the facts about the Reichstag Incendiarism, showing the unique mystery of the event.

The importance of the burning of the Reichstag lay not in the cause, but the use made of it by the Nazi leaders. It was evidently a great misfortune to their opponents; it allowed Hitler with a sudden spring to leap into power unchallenged, silencing and outlawing them. To his Allies, the Nationalists, it was unwelcome, as recent revelations have shown. In the steps which followed it, it was the Nazis who did and got everything, the Nationalists were left to look on.

Previous to February 26, 1933, the Headquarters of the Communists had been raided and searched, and masses of literature removed. The Chief of the Berlin Police, a Nationalist, had been retired to make place for a Nazi. On February 26, the *Conti*, a Government News Agency, reported discoveries for a Bolshevik revolt. False reports went out of fires caused by Communists. On February 27 Hitler, Göring and Goebbels were all back in Berlin from tours of speech-making in distant places. The subterranean passage from the official residence of Göring was used for bringing inflammable material to different parts of the Reichstag building; the fire occurred simultaneously in different parts of the building; this is strangely explained in Göring's statement as due to the Dutch Communist taken in the act going from one part to another with petrol and tearing parts of his garments to soak and ignite. Government announcements on February 24 of Communist plots were followed by release of the usual Reichstag guards on the night of the fire and no special precautions were taken. Documents alleged to incriminate Communists and others were promised immediate publication, but have never been produced; an inquiry and trial were to follow speedily; after two months no more is heard.

Hitler publicly expressed grim satisfaction that the seat of Republican Government had been laid low; he promised a public execution of the criminal who was not then even indicted for the crime. One cannot but admire the audacity and skill with which the event was exploited by Hitler. Nor can anyone wonder that few persons who have studied the conflicting statements should have found the official story incredible. There is sufficient to say that perhaps Hitler, Göring and Goebbels planned the fire, or were approving or profiting parties. There is certainly good reason for the Nazi leaders, who have professed themselves ready to do, and have done, greater crimes, to let the question of fire-guilt remain unsolved.

Without any question, suspicion and readiness to think that the fire was a Nazi plot are the prevailing opinions in many well-informed circles abroad.

The ex-Nazi, Dr. Emil Bell, who was pursued over the Austrian frontier by Brown Shirts, who murdered him near Kufstein and returned safe to German soil, was believed to have known more than anyone about the fire; his inner knowledge of Nazi methods caused his death.

Many searching examinations and offered solutions of the outrage have appeared in Foreign papers and especially in the *Manchester Guardian* of April 26 and 27, 1933, and the Paris *Le Journal* of April 5. See also Dr. Theodor Krämer's *Blut-März* 1933, published at Luxemburg.

CHAPTER XI

HITLER'S DICTATORSHIP

*No Nazi Mandate from the Voters—The Press and
the Dictatorship—Nazi Use of the Press—Ignorance
of Value of a Free Press—Nazi Fear of Foreign
Opinion—Instances of Disillusion*

NO NAZI MANDATE FROM THE VOTERS

THE votes polled on March 5, 1933, by the
various parties at the Reichstag Election (in
millions and omitting the "splinter parties"
polling less than a million votes each) show the
following:

Nazis (National Socialists) . .	over 17¼ millions
Nationalists Allied with Nazis .	over 3 millions
Social-Democrats (Socialists) .	over 7 millions
Communists	nearly 5 millions
Centre (Catholics) . . .	nearly 4½ millions
Bavarian People's Party . .	over 1 million

The Nazis polled about 47 per cent. of the
forty millions who went to the poll; they have
·used their alliance with the Nationalists to
assume all the power in the State for their
Leader Hitler. Significant facts of the voting
are that in spite of intense suppression the
Communists still polled nearly five millions,
though a million less than previously, and the
Social-Democrats nearly seven and a half

millions. The claim that the voting is a proof that all Germany wanted the Nazi policy slogan "All Power to Hitler" is disproved by the poll.

For the future, there appear to be millions who voted deliberately against Hitler; millions of voters supported the maintenance of the Republic, even though deprived of any press or public meeting propaganda or party organization possibilities and with thousands of their leading men in custody. This cannot mean security for Hitler if his plans miscarry. Opposition may be driven underground or sent into exile abroad; can it be, in Hitler's words, "utterly exterminated"?

THE PRESS AND THE DICTATORSHIP

The press has been cleverly used as well as constantly suppressed by the Nazis. The demands of the national aims and the dominance of a single party are quite incompatible with the theory that the press made "a fourth estate of the realm." In the theory and practice in France, U.S.A., the whole British Empire, and most civilized lands, the Newspaper Press must be allowed fair play and free liberty to report and criticize any event or saying of interest, so long as decency and freedom from libel or treason are excluded. The very antithesis to this theory is natural to Fascist States

and in lands under a Dictator's control, as
are Russia, Yugoslavia, Portugal, Italy and
Germany to-day. In these lands the press must
say nothing which the Government forbids and
utter no criticism which the Government finds
troublesome. In Germany the use of the press
as State organ and not a popular possession is
carried to extreme lengths. Telephone and
telegraph services are under spy-conditions;
the Broadcasting is under the Publicity and
Propaganda Department; of this Goebbels is
Minister in charge.

The authority to own or issue a newspaper
has been strictly circumscribed. As a result,
the whole aspect and character of the press of
Germany is changed from what it was a year
previous; the papers have the same titles, the
same get-up and their special features of Sport,
Drama, Music, etc.; but the public news and
political announcements, both as to home and
Foreign affairs, are in identical words, and
articles on national policy are just syndicated
communications from inspired Nazi headquarters. On such matters as are obviously not
of grave political issues, such as the regulations
for Sport, Lawn-Tennis Tournaments, Bathing
Costumes and Shopping in Department Stores,
on all these and many similar social activities
Hitler has his law to enforce; all is based on
the duty of "Cleansing the State."

NAZI USE OF THE PRESS

Hitler is the Leader and Dictator, who saved the State, and the Religious Prophet, awakening men's souls. To criticize him is sacrilege; to stand in his path is obstruction and treason. This being so, only those who are on Hitler's side should be allowed to preach in the pulpit, to teach in the school, to lecture in the university, to perform in theatre, opera or concert, to expound or defend the law in law-courts, or to sell goods in the shops. This accepted as word of the Leader it follows that tests of allegiance must be imposed or assumed from every one; but Marxists, Pacifists and Jews must have "no place in the National life." Great newspapers, like the *Berliner Tageblatt*, owned and staffed by Jews, and a moderate Liberal paper with a record and standing similar to that enjoyed by *The Times* or *Daily Telegraph* in London, was suddenly suppressed, soon appearing as a Nazi newspaper; the owners were forced out of the great undertaking at a price fixed by Germany's new rulers. Attacks on newspaper offices by Brown Shirts and ill-treatment of editors and damage to plant have been usual.

The freedom of the press has become a long-past memory in Germany: with it any sense of the duty to hear the other side. The press is now "to be forged into a tempered weapon of German policy, life and spirit." Syndicated articles and proper information are supplied with the desired results.

The Foreign Press especially of Switzerland, Scandinavia, France and Britain have enlightened Germany about what has been the course of German affairs and how the new regime is regarded. A number of Foreign papers are now excluded from Germany; to possess a copy of the *Manchester Guardian* may now mean serious consequences. The success of Hitler's press policy is seen in his having created in his admirers a satisfactory conviction that not a single life has been lost in the Revolution, which in fact "was no real revolution, but only a national awakening, since no blood was shed and no one has suffered anything; except perhaps those Communists who have burnt the Reichstag and would have started a massacre if they had not been put down." So writes a German lady to the present writer, and so millions of Germans are convinced.

IGNORANCE OF VALUE OF A FREE PRESS

Many Germans are contented with the changes which with swift completeness and fresh organization have been introduced. They do not yet realize what has been lost nor what altered circumstances are in front. Apart from the industrial outlook, the unemployment and commercial stagnation, the economic plans and aims of the Nazis may disturb many. Will the German Nation always tolerate a newspaper press less free to express independent views than that of Russia?

NAZI FEAR OF FOREIGN OPINION

Nazi nervousness about the press is shown by the frequent lecturings and protests of Göring to Foreign Journals and to the British Foreign Office for speeches made in Parliament, and to the assaults and apprehensions of Foreign journalists in Germany. Nazi representatives are sent to teach Nazi truth to countries deceived by Jewish atrocity propaganda. Dr. Thost, Hitler's special representative in London, spoke to M.P.s in a Committee Room of the House of Commons on April 26. Dr. Bogs, head of the Scandinavian section of the Nazi Press Department, on April 30, arrived in Copenhagen on a Scandinavian "Good Will" tour; his tactlessness and talk seemed to have been of doubtful value. On May 3 the German Government addressed a strong protest to Sweden against a speech of the Swedish Commerce Minister. In short, Nazis suppress news and opinions abroad, and resent in other nations any news and views not clearly labelled "Of Pure Nazi Origin."

INSTANCES OF DISILLUSION

The unanimous chorus of approval of Hitler's triumph and his boast "the whole nation behind him" soon began to change. The present writer submits three cases indicative of this from his own immediate and personal knowledge.

(*a*) A University Professor writes that though he welcomes for some reasons and had hopes of Hitler's advent to power, he must now admit that January 30, 1933, was a day of fate for Germany, that the treatment of the Jews is cruel and against the best German spirit, and that the changes being introduced into the Universities must lower German culture permanently.

(*b*) A lady writes to a friend in England an enthusiastic letter about the new life dawning in Germany, the absence of any outrages, injustices or disturbances, and asking English friends not to believe the Outrage Propaganda of Foreign Correspondents. Three weeks later, the same lady writes a very different letter from Swiss soil; she excuses her former letter as written partly in ignorant haste, but largely owing to the public appeals made in March 1933 that Germans should write to foreign friends to explain and defend the National Revolution. She names cases of ill-treatment in her own circle; she fears for a relative seeking a teaching post; she, being known as belonging to a liberal and pacifist circle, wants her former letter kept safe as she might have to require it as evidence if charged with disloyalty to Germany.

(*c*) The wife of a German Lutheran Pastor writes that as of foreign (though Aryan) birth she is made very uncomfortable and that her husband, an old Nationalist not a Nazi, has been strongly blamed for lukewarm prayers for Hitler.

In these three cases a reaction against the first enthusiasm for the result of the Reichstag Election is evident. The present writer could add from his personal experience other instances of the same kind.

CHAPTER XII

HITLER'S REIGN OF TERROR

A Real Reign of Terror—Violent Threats—Terror Employed to Compel Approval—Divergent Ideas of Terrorism—Excuses Easily Found for the Terror—Terrorism Extended into Remote Places—Hitler's Futile Appeal—The "D.A.Z." Protest—Irrefragable Evidence—Political Prisoners—Heartless Treatment of the Sick—Refugees Driven out of Germany—Grave Increase in "Suicides"—"Framed-up" Accusations Against High Officials—Many "Suicides" of Prisoners —A Typical Case: Frau Jankowski

A REAL REIGN OF TERROR

THERE IS a Reign of Terror in Germany, of course. Hitler founded his party on violence and has established his movement with professions and constant practice of illegal violence. His own example and teaching are full of violence. His written and spoken words seldom tend to conciliation or argument, but rather defiance and threatening. This surely needs no proof by any one who has read his autobiography or his party literature. The language repeatedly used by his chief partisans is so full of violence that were there no terror when the Nazis obtained power, they would have been fairly blamed for being braggarts afraid to strike. That they certainly are not. They have been recklessly daring in the brutality of their terror.

The prospect of terrorism with Hitler as Dictator was assured by the powerful success of Hitler's Private Army, the Brown Shirts (S.A. Sturm Abteilung) and his Defence Squadrons (Schutz-staffel, S.S.) A year before Hitler's Chancellorship these numbered 350,000 uniformed men; two months after the Election of March 5, 1933, they are claimed by Hitler to number 600,000. In 1931 and 1932 the papers of all parties, Right as well as Left, were full of the brutalities, illegalities, raids, robberies, assaults and beatings carried on by the Brown Shirts. Their efficiency as bandit battalions, under old army officers, being well supplied with arms, not always firearms ostentatiously displayed of course, and the Brown House buildings, barracks, "Lokale," and the complete organization and office information behind it all, made "a masterpiece of efficiency" (Mowrer, pp. 277 ff.). Hitler has himself preached and practised terrorism and brutality; he has also had the men to practise it. These have been taught to see and use terrorism.

VIOLENT THREATS

The violent incitement to lawless revenge and brutality of the speeches of Hitler and his leading supporters cannot be denied. Here are actual words used by these men:

Hitler (repeatedly uttered slogan) : "Heads will be rolling off; yes, heads will be rolling."

Goebbels: There will be hangings.

Gregor Strasser: We shall wade through blood up to
  our ankles.
Stöhr: Vice-President of the Reichstag: We shall give
  some work to the Hemp-industry.
Röver: We shall give the Ravens some feeding off the
  Marxists and Centre Party on the Gallows.
Dr. Frick: It will not be a bad thing when 10,000
  Marxist officials are ruined.

It is no wonder that terrorism is a method of
Government in Germany to-day. It would
have surprised those who know Germany, as it
has been below the surface of social life in
well-to-do quarters and away from quiet
holiday resorts, if there had been no terror.

TERROR EMPLOYED TO COMPEL APPROVAL

The Nazi Terror has taken three distinct
directions, against political opponents, pacificists, republicans and communists, also against
Jews, and also against the public generally to
drive everyone to be demonstrably on the
Nazi side. The campaign before the Brunswick
Elections, which was fully described in the
press, German as well as British, in September
1930, was a successful brutal dragooning of the
voters at Election time; by terrifying, bullying
and beating surprised voters they secured the
first Nazi majority for a provincial Landtag.
Hitler was himself in command of 60,000
Brown Shirts brought into Brunswick for the
Polling Day (September 14, 1930). Such an
imposing show of force, armed and well-

appointed men, with no apparent challenging forces, must have great weight with thousands.

DIVERGENT IDEAS OF TERRORISM

Suppose the British Government ordered that all policemen at Polling Stations on General Election Day should wear the Government's Party colours, that they should allow only party bills or literature of that party to be in evidence; this would be called Terrorism in Britain. In Germany such a procedure has to be expected; in fact, in aggravated form, since the Brown Shirts, when thus taken on in Government service, had long been known as party bullies and largely consisted of unemployed youths.

The question, What is exactly Terrorism? would be differently answered in Britain and Germany; what is tolerated, or excused abroad, is abominated and condemned by Britons.

EXCUSES EASILY FOUND FOR THE TERROR

The burning of the Reichstag appeared to justify the decrees of unlimited powers to "save the State from the Communist Menace." Seeing that the Communist doctrine preaches the use of force to establish the Rule of the Proletariat, the use of any extreme measures were accepted as quite right against "this Communist atrocity." After the peaceful day of the Election (March 5), the actions of the

Brown Shirts, under the direct incitement of Hitler and the Nazi leaders, developed into an intensified Reign of Terror. This is testified to by the Foreign press correspondents, with practical unanimity. The Terror was preached as a holy doctrine. Göring said on March 11, when speaking of his authority over the Prussian Police:

"I will use the police ruthlessly wherever the German people is being injured. An end must be put to the nonsense of every rogue being able to call on the police when he meets his deserts . . . the police are not there to protect rogues and vagabonds, swindlers, profiteers and traitors. . . . For years past we have told the people, 'you can settle accounts with the traitors.' We stand by our word. Accounts are being settled."

TERRORISM EXTENDED INTO REMOTE PLACES

Features of the Terror, especially horrible, were the extension of Brown Shirts' brutality into country and remote districts where Communists never had any hold, the raids of rough Nazis to pay off personal grudges, to rob and damage quiet homes and to indulge in beating and kidnapping, all to an extent never before seen. Heines, a notorious murderer, amnestied and lauded for his patriotism by Hitler, was at the head of a campaign in Silesia; women were not respected, their hair cut off and stripped of clothing, dragged from home and beaten, such things excused if the House-father was a Reichsbanner (Republican Guard) man. The Terror which began in a political battle in civil war conditions became a reign of robbery and bloodshed at the will and pleasure of Brown Shirt boys.

HITLER'S FUTILE APPEAL

That there was this real and terrible state of things is attested by Hitler himself. On March 10 he issued an appeal to his Nazis to "refrain from molesting individuals or disturbing business life." "The honour and safety of Germany was entrusted to them!" Göring immediately qualified this by urging them to "settle accounts with the traitors." The Nazi *Beobachter* published Hitler's appeal in small, Göring's words in big type. The persons who write to the British papers or to friends from Germany declaring that no outrages have occurred and that they never saw any atrocities may very well be speaking literal truth. The Terror was not one of Street fighting, barricades in the streets or squares, big buildings held by insurgents till destroyed by bombs or burning. Such terrors have been seen in Dublin not many years ago; what happened, for a few weeks in Ireland only, causes still grief and shame to many, but was never proclaimed as a permanent policy. But the Nazi Terror was, and is intended to remain, a terror of baser and more abiding evil. It is not seen everywhere; even granted that it was necessary to start it, why should it be continued when Nazi domination is triumphant? Why should its existence in the past as well as to-day be denied, when it was promised for years by Hitler himself, and is being constantly urged and threatened as the basis of the National life?

THE "D.A.Z." PROTEST

The great Berlin Newspaper *D.A.Z.* (*Deutsche Allgemeine Zeitung*) occupies a position in some ways like that of the London *Morning Post*; conservative, correct, Nationalist, Capitalistic, it has close touch with Nationalist colleagues in Hitler's Cabinet. This paper published an article on March 13, 1933, just a week after the Election, which contained these words:

"In wide circles the panic terror has spread. This may now be allayed. The Chancellor's manifesto is of decisive importance . . . the administrative authorities and the police . . . often did not dare to intervene against disturbers of the peace . . . they wrongly assumed that some responsible quarter might cover the activities of irresponsible juvenile 'flying squads.' . . . Premises in which 'political prisoners' arrested by private persons are confined must, if not already known to the police, be notified to the authorities. . . . Private revenge in blood must no longer be taken, etc."

This testimony of a paper favouring the Hitler power admits that a Terror existed, that it was extending and especially that these features were prevalent—Juvenile flying squads left alone by the Police, Houses disturbed, Persons arrested without warrant to be confined in places not known to the police, and private revenge in blood. That a Terror existed in intensified and unjustified form in Germany during March 1933 is an admitted and established fact. It may be boasted about by Göring and Goebbels, though presumably it was not welcomed by Neurath, von Papen and Hugenberg, the leading Nationalists in the Cabinet, and indignantly denied at German Embassies and Consulates.

IRREFRAGABLE EVIDENCE

Against Germans who declare with amazing effrontery, as the German Ambassador lately in London and Herr Schacht in New York, that there were no Terror and no outrages in Germany, there are three convincing proofs to the contrary; the thousands of political prisoners in prisons and camps in Germany; the thousands of refugees who have escaped from Germany on every border, and the Anti-semite Jew-baiting policy of Hitler's Dictatorship. Each of these facts prove that the Terror has existed, still continues with ferocity and is part of Hitler's programme.

POLITICAL PRISONERS

The numbers of political prisoners in Germany whose present detention dates from the intensive terror of the pre-Election days has never been stated by the Government. But undoubtedly the number must far exceed 10,000 and probably is not less than 30,000. The Government disingenuously says, first, that they are settling up accounts with the traitors, and then that they are temporarily placed under "preventive arrest" (Schutzhaft). The arrest is *preventive* in a triple sense: from conspiring against the Government; from being hurt by the indignant Germans, who are now the Nation up in arms against the traitors in their midst; and from allowing even their families to know where they are imprisoned! With no authority beyond the word of the leading man of the Brown Shirt gang who arrests, no charge in legal form, no right to be heard in Court of Law and with no assertion of citizen's rights (no procedure like British *Habeas Corpus*), many leading politicians, journalists, Reichstag Members and others have been hurried away and with no promise of release. Just before Easter 1933 the Cardinal Archbishop of Munich appealed to General von Epp, the Nazi Statthalter (Vice-regent) of Bavaria, to allow "fathers of families at least" and "even if only on leave" to celebrate Easter at home. Over 1,000 were released in response. It was officially stated that the new concentration camp created at Dachau in Bavaria would be for 5,000 and that another Bavarian Camp was projected. In every part of Germany prisons are full;

institutional buildings and camps with barbed wire surrounds are occupied. It is understood that food conditions and exercise, occupation and recreation facilities are not bad, general conditions, on the whole, compare favourably with those in the prisons for political opponents in Russia. The intention seems to be to keep men and women in detention for years, with forced labour, till submissive acquiescence is induced. On the other hand, it is established that many political opponents have been arrested, been beaten, tortured, not infrequently landed in dangerous state in hospital, and driven to sign documents that they had been well treated and would in future support the Nazi State, etc.

HEARTLESS TREATMENT OF THE SICK

The authorities of the political prisons in Prussia, when requested to allow sick prisoners and certain other hard cases to be considered with a view to a release or to permit friends taking places as hostages for those released, replied that no priority of any sort would be granted, and that those for whom petitions were sent in would be placed last in rotation for any consideration or release.

What exactly will be the policy of Hitler towards the Marxists, his political opponents, those "traitors and blackguards," whose heads he would roll off when he reached power, and whose "Marxism" must be utterly destroyed in

Germany? Concentration Camps and Labour Colonies, in which bread for work and a minimum wage would encourage the inmates to a sensible loyalty to National-Socialism, are now started. But will such methods convince the seven million voters, Social-Democrats, and five million, Communists, who voted against Hitler in face of the terror of March 1933, and make them proud and loyal Nazis?

REFUGEES DRIVEN OUT OF GERMANY

There are thousands of Refugees from Germany in every country surrounding the German Reich. Of these 50,000 are of Jewish blood; many are politicians and pacifists who have fled from the conditions of terror and menace within the Reich. Some may indeed have fled in panic; some even may be now returning to risk the dangers in their own country, which they left in haste and without means; if funds are exhausted and supplies cut off, they may choose to suffer ills they know and not fly to others that they know not. There were certainly over 1,500 Refugees in the Saar in April 1933, and the estimate was that 3,000 were in Paris, three or four thousand in Switzerland; more had plans and hopes for further journeying from German soil than intentions to return.

Anti-Hitlerite newspapers in German are appearing in Prague and Copenhagen; it is possible that an anti-Hitler influence will be growing up with exiled Germans directing it

in every land in Europe in which the love of
the Fatherland will survive when devotion to
Hitler in Germany fades.

There are other signs of the times in this
movement of the peoples. When Russia threw
off its Czardom in 1917, there was at once, and
continued for years, a stream of Russians
seeking to return to Russia. Nothing is heard of
the great numbers of Germans in other lands
having any desire or plans to return to Germany.
The Auslands-deutschen (Germans abroad) are
many and loyal to German language, habits
and sentiment; have they responded to the
Third Reich? Again, the friendly and generous
way in which German Refugees have been
treated, both officially by frontier and police
authorities and by individuals and organized
societies in France pre-eminently and in
Britain as well as in other lands, must impress
even the proud self-confidence of Hitler.

GRAVE INCREASE IN "SUICIDES"

Suicides in Germany have been a grave and
saddening feature in the national life for ten
years before 1933. The inflation brought many
thousands of the middle-class, professional and
intellectual families, pensioners, elderly persons,
rentiers and others to absolute want and
starvation; suicide offered to a society in
despair the end of an unbearable lot. Since
1919, suicide has been so common in Germany
that Hitler asserts that from distress and

misery 224,900 persons (over 300 weekly) have taken their lives since Peace was signed. Greatly increased unemployment, taxation and cost of living, a reduction of "the Dole" pittance and of all pensions in the world slump, maintained conditions inviting suicide. Since the Nazi Terror was established, the number of suicides has been swollen by the panic among the Jews; this has driven young students and married women as well as professional men, driven from Law Courts, Hospitals, or Teaching posts, to consider what seemed the only thing left.

Many suicides have been recorded in the German press; in *The Times* and foreign newspapers readers have been accustomed to a monotonous recurrence of suicide cases.

"FRAMED-UP" ACCUSATIONS AGAINST HIGH OFFICIALS

In the months of March and April the Nazi terror developed a new Campaign against prominent public men for alleged "robbery," "fraud," "embezzlements" and "misappropriation of public funds" in connection with the public undertakings and contracts entered into by municipalities, public-utility undertakings and public companies; any leading man, not a Nazi or Nationalist, became at once liable for the false charges, framed-up evidence, immediate imprisonment and judgment before a Court, where the avowed object was (as in

the Moscow trial of Metro-Vickers' engineers)
to assert the objects and interest of the State.
Such sweeping charges and the Law Courts of
Germany as now employed have driven such
accused men to suicide; they knew that certain
and cruel revenge was awaiting them as part
of Hitler's will to utterly destroy Marxism and
make the life of a German Social-Democrat
impossible.

MANY "SUICIDES" OF PRISONERS

A number of suicides are reported as occurring
in prisons and detention camps. Strong suspicions are aroused when such statements are
made. A leading Bavarian Communist, a
member of the Bavarian Landtag, Dressel,
opened his wrist artery in the Dachau Concentration Camp; five similar cases were
reported in one day (May 10, 1933); persons
committing suicide who are said by their
friends to be of such character as to give doubt
to the allegations.

These cases may be really voluntary self-
intended deaths. They are certain proof that
a terror exists. When prisoners commit suicide,
they are terrified, and when they do this in
many cases there is a rule of Terror. The same
applies to the many cases where prisoners are
reported as "shot dead when trying to escape."
The friends of these men believe that the
usual explanation "suicide" is a euphemism for
"killed in cold blood."

H

A TYPICAL CASE: FRAU JANKOWSKI

Many outrages have been circumstantially given in newspapers in every country except Germany. Here is a notorious and indubitable case of gross brutality—that of Frau Marie Jankowski. She was taken from her home in Köpenick in the early hours of March 21 by 14 men in Nazi uniform, bearing carbines and revolvers; brought to the Nazi quarters in Dorotheenstrasse, Berlin; stripped of clothes and called on to declare the Republican flag shown to her "a foul flag," before some 20 Nazis present; she refused; the leading Nazi then ordered "20 stripes"; stripped and thrown on a table she was held there and received repeated beatings, "at least 100 strokes"; she rolled bleeding on the floor; she was taken downstairs and left in the street. Her husband complained next day to the Police, who said that they were powerless. Frau Jankowski is well known as a municipal and social worker, active in the distribution of relief; she is a Socialist. The case was fully investigated by *The Times* Berlin Correspondent who saw her in Hospital, and given in *The Times* (April 1, 1933). It led to an official statement that an inquiry would be made, but nothing further is known of the matter.

When Herr Bogs, the Hitler Scandinavian Envoy, was asked about the case at his press audience in Copenhagen, he replied, "If any Communist ever deserved a good thrashing, it was Frau Jankowski!"

Statements in this chapter, and especially in those made in the concluding paragraphs, are partly based on information given to the author by men and women whom he cannot distrust; these persons all asserting the existence of Terrorism as an essential part of Hitler's regime. One of these witnesses is a professional man of European reputation, who is already in the service of one foreign country and is offered a leading position by one of the Great Powers. In April 1933 he was waiting to join his wife and children, whose departure from Germany to join him was causing him natural anxiety.

CHAPTER XIII

HITLER'S PERSECUTION OF THE JEWS

German Anti-Semitism—Russian Anti-Semitism Condemned—Hitler's Race Fanaticism—Stock Arguments Against the Jews—Many Cruelties on Jews— Many Recorded Cases—Hitler's Immediate Attack on Jews—Civilization Shocked—Nazi Cruelty Stirs the World—The Boycott of April 1—The Boycott Failed, Private Vengeance Increased—"No Jew a Member of the Nation"—Germany's Cultural Losses

GERMAN ANTI-SEMITISM

ANTI-SEMITISM has had a long history in Germany. It existed before 1096 when Peter the Hermit preached with fiery zeal the First Crusade; one of Peter's armies pursued a course of Jew-killing in the Rhineland towns and butchered 10,000 Jews. Jew-baiting has been an endemic ailment of the German race for centuries. In 1879 Berlin seethed in an agitation which amazed and disgusted Europe— the *Judenhetze*, led by the notorious Court Preacher Stöcker.

"Under his auspices the years 1880–81 became a period of bitter conflicts with the Jews. The Conservatives supported Stöcker . . . the Lutheran Clergy followed suit . . . the Ultramontanes (Catholics) readily adopted Anti-semitism . . . a formidable body of public opinion was thus recruited for the Anti-semites. Violent debates took place in the Prussian Diet. A petition to exclude the Jews from schools, universities and from public offices was presented to Bismarck. Jews were boycotted

and insulted. Duels, often fatal, became of daily occur-
rence. Unruly demonstrations and street riots were
reported. Pamphlets attacking . . . Jewish life streamed
in hundreds from the press. . . . The Liberals adopted
such a strong attitude that the agitation failed to obtain
legislative sanction. The Crown Prince (afterwards the
Emperor Frederick and the Crown Princess, the British
Princess Royal) boldly headed a party of protest, publicly declaring that the agitation was 'a shame and a
disgrace to Germany.' The following Reichstag Election
in 1881 showed a declining power in the agitation"
(*Encl. Brit.*, Art. on Anti-semitism). Nevertheless a strong
often violent anti-semitism of Germany persisted, though
since 1881 it played little political importance. There
were two schools, economic and ethnological, according
as ideals of Christian Socialism or Racial Purity dominated. But Anti-semitism was never absent from large
sections of the people, and it flourished especially among
ignorant religious circles and among freak theorists and
pseudo-scientists. Until Hitler arose, to the rich Reactionary and Capitalist parties, the Social Democrat was
the enemy, whose alliance with the Centre (Catholics)
made them glad to have in defence of the existing order
both the wealthy Jews of finance and business and the
strongly individualist Jews of the middle-classes. The
Judenhetze of Hitler must be alien to the instincts and
ideas, as it is to the traditions, of his Nationalist Allies,
but awakes ideas which had been slumbering for years.

RUSSIAN ANTI-SEMITISM CONDEMNED

In 1914 when the War broke out the German
nation was united against Russia, because
Russia was held to be a barbarous, ignorant
and brutal power; the Russian power had
incited pogroms, led by the police, against
the cultured Jews. When in September 1914
German Armies entered Poland, special appeals

signed by the German High Command (Hitler's friend, Ludendorff) offered to the Jews
" . . . justice and freedom: equality of civil rights, freedom of faith, freedom of work undisturbed in all branches of economic and cultural life in your own spirit. . . . As friends we come to you. . . . Equal rights for Jews shall be developed upon firm foundations . . . " etc.

The dignified protest of the German Republican Government to the Peace Conference in May 1919, which has never been attacked by any German party or statesman, said:

"Germany advocates in principle the protection of national minorities. . . . Germany on her part is resolved to treat minorities of alien origin in her territories . . . fairly on such principles."

Again, when in May 1922 a German Polish Convention was made to assure proper administration in the German-Polish districts, Article 66 ran as follows:

"The German Government undertakes to grant to all inhabitants full and complete protection of life and liberty without distinction of birth, nationality, language, race or religion. . . ." And Article 67 reasserts "the same civil and political rights without distinction of race, language or religion, etc."

These events of 1914, 1919 and 1922, never then or since denounced, show that the national feeling was not anti-Jewish. It is Hitler's fanatical race-hatred and marvellous gift of inspiring a religious fervour and a blind belief in himself; those who follow him have made anti-Judaism a violent movement in Germany. Hitler's fanatical race-hatred and its religious complex can be seen in these extracts from his autobiography (*My Struggle*):

HITLER'S RACE FANATICISM

"If the Jew wins . . . his crown of victory is the death-wreath of humanity, and this planet will again, as it did ages ago, float through the ether, bereft of man. . . . When I defend myself against the Jews I fight for the work of the Lord."

"The black-haired Jewish youth lies for hours in ambush, a Satanic joy in his face, for the unsuspecting girl whom he pollutes with his blood and steals from her own race. . . . By every means he seeks to wreck the racial bases of the nation . . . he deliberately befouls women and girls . . . it was and is the Jew who brought negroes to the Rhine, brought them with the . . . intent to destroy the white races . . . by persistent bastardiza-tion, to hurl it from the . . . heights it has reached . . . he deliberately seeks to lower the race-level by steady corruption of the individual. . . ."

These quotations from Hitler's book are typical of his oratory which has been described as sermonic and inspiring.

STOCK ARGUMENTS AGAINST THE JEWS

As the Hitler press and his admirers have persistently repeated such extraordinary things, a list of some of them must be given, with proper corrections.

(a) That since the War thousands of Eastern Jews have entered Germany from the lands East of Germany and greatly increased the burden of aliens of a lower culture and standard of life.

This cannot be the full truth, since the last official census available showed that in 1925, compared with the previous pre-War census (1910), the percentage of Jews in the Reich had fallen from 9·3 to 9 per cent.

In round figures the German population is over 61 million, and of these under 570,000 are Jews. That many Jews have come from Poland and Galicia is answered by the fact that Jews previously under German rule in Poland, and under Austrian rule in Poland and Galicia have left lands where as Germans they would now be under alien rules, language and government; they were German previously, and now under the same conditions as the other German exiles from those lands they have with these shown preference for Germany by coming over the new German frontiers.

To represent these former German subjects as low-class foreigners is a mean and unworthy falsehood.

(b) That the Jews refused to serve in the Army in the War (Goebbels).

Twelve thousand German Jews served in Germany's forces, and this was over 2 per cent. of the total Jew population. *Died,*

(c) That they have plotted and planned the murder of Hitler. This has been the burden of pamphlets sold by Brown Shirts in the streets of Berlin.

This lie will hardly be believed in Germany and not at all in any other country. No attempt has yet been recorded on Hitler's life.

(d) That the Jews are all traitors to the Germans among whom they lived and in every way helped and encouraged the French and their Allies to ruin Germany by the War and the Peace Treaties.

This is a vague and extravagant statement which surely needs no answer. It is surely as impossible of proof as the extravagant statements made by an English writer in a series of books that Communism is a Jewish national conspiracy to ruin all non-Jews and destroy Britain!

(e) That learning, law, art, poetry and science proceeding from Jews must be false and degrading and all books, pictures, music and science connected with Jews must be eliminated.

This doctrine is seriously believed, extraordinary as it appears to men of education in other lands. A Doctor of Berlin University writes to the author, justifying the treatment of Einstein and the confiscation of his bank credits, on the ground that Einstein is a scientific fraud, whom a Jewish press campaign had given a perfectly fraudulent fame and that he was getting off very cleverly by being welcomed in Paris and Madrid. The mad *furor* of Hitlerism seen in such German letters is typical of much in Hitler's terror. (It may prove that the writer of the tirade against Einstein who deplored a year ago the huge vote obtained against Hindenburg by Hitler may have written this under fear of losing a post dependent upon Government.)

Several Jewish German Scientists have received the Nobel prize. On its award they were paraded as instances of proud German culture. To-day they are ejected from their posts or allowed to resign!

(*f*) That Jews by their influential positions in politics, in the press and in the public services had deliberately betrayed the German nation and brought it to the desperate condition which Hitler had changed into the security and prosperity of the Third Reich.

This serious charge has imposed on many because without any doubt many Germans have risen to eminence since the War in the Reichstag as Members of Coalition Cabinets working under what Hitler denounces as "The System"; also in the press, both as journalists and newspaper-owners; and in administrative posts in public services (cf. Mowrer, p. 231).

But this only means that Jews provided many clever men who tried with success to work the Republic. Only if working "The System" was treachery can this charge be established. It also assumes another falsehood, that the many other politicians, pressmen and officials, though not Jews, were not guilty to the same degree, though more in numbers; this assumption would appear to imply that the Jews in these careers were superior to the others of pure German blood.

(*g*) That the Jews have invented, and profited by, the Financial Scandals and Municipal Profiteering which have been notorious in post-War Germany.

This is a specious and widespread accusation which has this to be said for it; the War period and early post-War years were marked by gross profiteering and

an increase of corrupt dealings. This was seen in un-
doubted German magnates like Stinnes, the Thyssen
and Krupp concerns, not only with Jewish financiers.
The Barmat Brothers, who swindled the Prussian State
Bank, were Jews. But Matthias Erzberger, a great
Catholic, was condemned by a Berlin Court for Parliamentary corruption.

In the early confusion and poverty of the post-War
Republic, temptations and opportunities were numerous.
Yet the disclosures in Germany were mild compared
with the "graft" and corruption in New York, Chicago
and some Canadian cities. In many lands, even in England,
with its Hatry scandal, there have been commercial
scandals with disgrace in which many Gentiles were
involved.

The framed-up accusations against political opponents
have already been described (p. 112, ante), and the same
Nazi processes of law as a party and political campaign
are in progress against Jewish concerns.

MANY CRUELTIES ON JEWS

The Jews have been, and still are being,
attacked by various refinements of cruelty. The
Nazi Terror renders many Jewish homes and
lives intolerable by raids, robberies, assaults
and kidnapping; at the hands of the Brown
Shirt detachments such actions are so frequent,
unexpected and so abominable as to drive to
madness or suicide many innocent non-Aryans.
Such treatment on human beings by Government agents in Germany would, if perpetrated
on dogs or cats in England, be followed by
heavy fines or imprisonment. These cases are
numerous; many have been recounted in the
press; far more remain without any public notice.

MANY RECORDED CASES

The record of known cases given by the booklet *J'Accuse*, published by World Alliance for Combating Anti-Semitism, does not profess to give all cases that have occurred, and as the proceedings of the Jew-baiters continue the sum of cruelty mounts up. (British Empire Headquarters, 33 St. James's Street, S.W. 1.)

On April 11, 1933, a well-known lawyer of Chemnitz, Dr. Weiner, who had served in the War and risen from the ranks to be Captain, was taken from his home by Nazis in uniform; these men produced a document authorizing his arrest, which Dr. Weiner told his wife before leaving was in order. He went without resistance; and his body was found next day in the country, dead from bullet wounds. A police statement was issued that no order had been issued for his arrest to the Nazis, and that the abductors were "criminals in Nazi uniform." So far as is known no regret or compensation has been offered to the widow and no inquiry instituted. Dr. Weiner, as having served in the War, was legally exempt from the decree or police orders of the Government against the Jews.

This case is but one of the outrages which can be described on good evidence and amount to many hundreds. It is hard to believe that any civilized Government would pursue such a policy, which at one moment denies, at another boasts of its success and continuance, and at another admits and passes over as the works of criminals.

HITLER'S IMMEDIATE ATTACK ON JEWS

The Campaign against Judaism was started on Hitler's becoming Chancellor. In February 1933, weeks before the Reichstag Election (March 5, 1933), the "purifying of Germany" from Jewish contamination began. Doctors were dismissed from public service, teachers

from their schools, lawyers from the Law
Courts, whether there as Attorneys (Rechtsan-
wälte) or Judges, and many from administrative posts in public offices. Business houses were
induced to dismiss Jews on their staffs. Contracts for supplies to Hospitals, Institutions and
Stores were taken from firms with any Jewish
taint or contact. Strict conditions were imposed
to safeguard any business house, using any
"non-Aryan" support, from having Government business connection.

This widespread plan to eliminate Jewish
elements from German life was of course not
carried through in a day or even in a month.
It began as one of the first sweeping changes;
it must be admitted that in thoroughness,
steady persistence and uninterrupted force it
was ruthless and brutal; it fulfilled the Fascist
law that "Brutality is a moral righteous thing,
if it is sudden, stern and establishing firmly the
new order."

From the Nazi standpoint it was grand.

CIVILIZATION SHOCKED

The general feeling of decency and humanity
which binds nations together in a recognized
standard of civilization was shocked by this
revival of mediæval persecution. A war of
religion is now no longer tolerable. A national
revival of laws for slave-holding and slave-
selling would be regarded as a shame to the

nation and a menace to civilization. Hitler, with intense conviction of his righteous mission, never understood the solidarity of humanity. He defied humanity by declaring that there was no cruelty in this purging the German nation of a criminal race, which as aliens had brought ruin on Germany. The protests and public indignation abroad were all due to the Outrage Propaganda of Jews who had got at the sensation-loving lying foreign press. This was a diplomatic reproach for a German regime which would reassert the honour of the nation and make Germany respected once more. It set the world against Hitler. But it made him a greater hero than ever with his infatuated Nazis; it gave a new excuse for violence and terrorism. In March the bullying raids of the Brown Shirts were intensified and a panic against the Jews was encouraged.

NAZI CRUELTY STIRS THE WORLD

Circumstantial cases of the Jewish Terror in March 1933 are reported in most papers in every country outside Germany. The following from the *Manchester Guardian* (March 27, 1933) is typical of many: "Three Jews were arrested by Brown Shirts in the Café New York, taken in a car (number known) to the S.A. "Lokal" in Wallnertheaterstrasse, where they were robbed of several hundred marks, beaten bloody with truncheons and turned out semi-conscious in the street. On the same day four Jews were taken to a Nazi S.A. "Lokal" in the Schillingerstrasse, robbed of 400 marks and beaten bloody till they fainted."

THE BOYCOTT OF APRIL I

Nazi savagery against "Juda" was terrible indeed for all Jews in Germany; but the world-wide disgust and distrust of the new German regime was serious for Hitler. He decided to start as from April 1, 1933, a national and permanent Boycott of all Jew shops and other business houses, including Cafés and Restaurants, etc. This was to be carried out as long as the foreign press published atrocity-lies about the Nazis.

Preparations were made in every city and town where Jews were well established to organize the Boycott. Before the day full notices were given. Pamphlets and press announcements, proclamations and speeches, told the people not to buy from the Jews, but only from Germans. Jewish shops and restaurants were marked with huge yellow placards or paint on the windows to warn the public; the shop assistants were officially informed that they must not assist the proprietors to sell, but were entitled to claim full pay, etc., for days ahead. At the doors of all Jew-owned concerns on Saturday, April 1, stood Brown Shirts who prevented persons from entering unless entrance was insisted on; if they entered, they would be photographed and their portraits shown at the Cinema in the evening; such sensational conditions attracted thousands to the streets;

their orderly behaviour, with no riot or
violent damage to Jewish concerns, was in
welcome contrast to the anti-Semitism of pre-
war days; this being borne in mind gave the
Nazis their occasion to boast that they pro-
tected the Jews from an indignant public and
that the tales of Nazi outrages against the Jews
were obviously fabrications. The Jewish Boycott was especially directed against the large
department stores, where the low prices, wide
choice and spacious galleries had for years
been one of the attractions to Berlin visitors and
inhabitants. The Nazis have always been
hostile to such stores in their anxiety to
gain the small shop-keepers of the whole
country.

THE BOYCOTT FAILED, PRIVATE VENGEANCE INCREASED

The great national Boycott lasted one day.
On the next it was announced in various Nazi
organs that it had been such a success that the
foreign press atrocity-lies were answered and
would cease; that it would be resumed after
three days: that it was a dress rehearsal for the
permanent boycott which would follow; that
though it was a success and would be followed
to complete elimination of Jewish shops, yet
it was necessary to go steadily, every end could
not be immediately attained. The net result
was that it was never publicly resumed; the

failure of the Boycott was evident; the Nazi Terror had aroused Jewish sympathies in every land and had stirred the Jewish community from the Rothschilds, the Lords of high finance, to the poor Jews of the London East End to united protest and inauguration of relief plans. The question became one of the first importance in the British Parliament and Foreign Embassies. Hitler had shown his splendid organizing abilities, and the perfect working of his machine; he had soon in hand other ways of "cleaning the nation from its non-Aryan pollution." He had lowered himself and Germany in the regard of the world; he would take compensation by a fresh procedure against his Jewish fellow-citizens.

"NO JEW A MEMBER OF THE NATION"

The conditions under which Jews are now placed in Germany are in full accordance with the 5th Point of the Nazi Programme; "No Jew may be a Member of the Nation"; therefore Jews have no civil rights. Their passports have been taken from them; yet they are ·prevented from emigrating, ostensibly because they would wage war against Germany more easily from without its borders. They may hold no public offices and are excluded from schools and universities either as teachers or learners. Millions of marks have been lost by the Jews by confiscation of their properties or shares in businesses, by loss of pay, pensions, offices, and prospects, by the forcible transfer of such undertakings as great newspaper and publishing concerns (like the Mosse firm); the losses apart from ruin to homes and injuries to body, mind and estate, can never be estimated. The injustice of all this has moved many thousands abroad, while to Germans it is a mere trifle compared with the injustices which the nation have suffered for the past twenty years. The Nazi Terror against the Jews is a world-tragedy; it is nothing less than a high-wall barrier between the great German nation and the rest of Western Civilization.

GERMANY'S CULTURAL LOSSES

The deaths of fifty Jews are recorded, with names, circumstances and addresses in the booklet issued by the World Alliance; this list, giving only some of the martyrs to their racial caste, include eminent men like the famous publisher of Berlin, Ulstein, who was officially stated to have died from "natural causes" though he never recovered consciousness from the beating of Nazis who broke into his house. Deaths and tortures, as well as robberies and deprivation of high positions, and the means of earning a livelihood, cannot be instigated and rewarded by the Government of any country without a lowering of the moral sense of the whole community.

The intellectual and cultural, scientific and artistic losses are incalculable. Eight Nobel Prizemen for Science, Nobel Prizemen in other ranks, and many leading musicians, artists and literary men, at least four of the writers whose works have been "best-sellers" in England, France and England, great figures in the world of theatre and opera, like Bruno Walter and Max Reinhardt, men who a year ago were honoured and named to foreigners as giving proud distinction to German culture, are suddenly declared unfit for "purified and revived Germany." Insulted and spat on by Nazis, who are lauded as "the brave and noble young Germans!" This would be considered incredible were it not defended by Ambassadors and Diplomats of Germany in the capitals of Europe as well as recorded in organs of the Press, previously considered Pro-German and acknowledged as non-sensational and reliable sources of general information.

The poetry of Heine and the performance of Lessing's great classic drama *Nathan der Weise* are no longer delights of every cultured German, but abominations to be rooted out by taking from the Libraries all copies of these works, to be replaced by Hitler's *My Struggle*.

When fanaticism driven to such mad excess possesses a nation and evokes no protest from any voice that can reach the world outside, Germans must not expect anything but the verdict that Hitler's triumph means the end of the finest and most admired elements of German culture.

The ablest men in law, medicine and business being driven by hundreds from Law Courts, Hospitals and offices and great concerns can only mean the lowered standing of Germany among the nations.

[This chapter has not attempted to give an exhaustive picture of all the phases of the Persecution of the German Jews. It has attempted to show some aspects of it which non-Germans forget and others which Germans ignore. The author is indebted for information on this subject to two publications, which should be read by any who wish to gain fuller knowledge of the Anti-Semitism of Germany to-day.

The Persecution of the Jews in Germany, published by the Joint Foreign Committee of the Board of Deputies of British Jews and the Anglo-Jewish Association, April

1933 . . . and *J'Accuse*, published by the Alliance for Combating Anti-Semitism.

Some documents of Nazi instructions and some statistics of grave nature are given, with much other material in Paul Kreglinger's "Judenverfolgung in Deutschland" (Utrecht, 1933).]

CHAPTER XIV

HITLER'S PROGRAMME

*Rapid Progress—Hitler's Future—Foreign Policy—
Frontier Dangers—Danzig, Saar, Austria—Unifi-
cation of the Reich—Hohenzollern Monarchy Less
Likely—Return of Reigning Princes Unlikely— Land
Policy—Hitler's Socialism—No Trades Unions
Allowed—Religion and Art—Health and Race Purity
—Sport—No Jews in "National" Sport—Education
Policy—Universities Under Hitler—Holocaust of Non-
German Books—Legal Rights and Procedure—No
"Objectivity or Equality Before the Law"*

RAPID PROGRESS

HITLER has established his Dictatorship with
astonishing rapidity and with apparent security.
The terrorism of his actions against "Marxist"
political opponents and Jews has sown seeds
of possible future danger, but has not weakened him at home. He has silenced all criticism
in the German press. By his consummately
managed propaganda at home, as conspicuously successful as his propaganda abroad has
been futile, he has removed all doubt and
hesitation. He has made a beginning of many
changes. For his Four-Year Plan he has foundations already laid and enough to occupy the
energies of his people.

HITLER'S FUTURE

The dangers before Hitler may be briefly considered. First, what if death or resignation removed the aged Hindenburg from the Presidency of Germany? In all probability Hitler would become President, retaining all the power he now holds and his status and dignity enhanced. This would guard him against the possibility of a split in the Nazi movement. When the Nationalists in its ranks are shed or absorbed, will it go more to the left or the right? Will the Nazis become a party in which von Papen would be at home, or one in which Göring would be fully content? In brief, will Hitler keep the reactionary aristocrat with his landed power, strong capitalist leanings and a restored monarchy in his front ranks? Or will his programme's promises of a land policy as radical as Mr. Lloyd George's in 1909 and of the full Socialism of the National-Socialist Party sweep all before it? The latter seems to be more natural to Hitler, provided unforeseen events do not vitally change the conditions now prevailing in Central Europe. Can the economic decline of the World be relieved by the decisions of the London World Economic Conference? If not, what will be the position of Germany as the greatest industrial country in Europe?

Will Germany be the greatest sufferer in the

further collapse? And if the collapse becomes a general chaos, will Germany survive its present anxious stability? To these questions the German would reply that Germany, when divided and drifting in policy and without strong leadership, has suffered, and survived, more than any other European State, and she can suffer more readily, and withstand more safely than other states, the storm of international chaos.

FOREIGN POLICY

What of Hitler's Foreign Policy? Is it for War or Peace? Here is an immense problem, with great possibilities. Some may fear that a preventive war by Poland would be easier now than a resort to arms a few years hence. Germany will be then, with air force and fully equipped army, a very uncomfortable neighbour. Of course Mussolini, the patron and model of Hitler, has made his militarist speeches and policy more to impress and dominate his own nation than to threaten peace. Mussolini has played a leading and sincere part in the struggle to reach Disarmament at Geneva.

Neither Italy nor Britain will permit any war in Central Europe. Hitler's policy has been stated to include a good understanding with Britain and Italy, revision of the Peace Treaties, and economic development towards the East. The cool attitude to France, the Hitlerite earlier repudiation of Locarno, and the challenge to The League of Nations are unpromising. Yet, peace is at present essential to Hitler's aims, and even to his existence. This he knows. His authority must enforce a peaceful policy on his proud and belligerent forces.

FRONTIER DANGERS

Frontier incidents on every side and arrests and ill-treatment of foreign nationals on German soil have been painfully frequent. Brown Shirts have dashed in their cars into Austria or Lichtenstein, Alsace or Poland to kidnap, murder or rob and to return unscathed and uncensured to their German quarters. Hitler can afford to curb frontier incidents which may if continued be a serious obstacle to peace.

DANZIG, SAAR, AUSTRIA

These are three adjacent regions where the Nazi movement affords a grave problem for Hitler, in Danzig, the Saar, and Austria. . . . Danzig was made a free city and placed at the mercy of a bitterly hostile Poland, in defiance of the Fourteen Points; the Election of a Danzig Diet at the end of May 1933 may see the Nazis in power to challenge Poland, to threaten peace, and even to call in Hitler to rule. . . . In the Saar, which has suffered under a Commission appointed by the League of Nations, the inhabitants are loyal Germans and await the plebiscite promised them for 1935 to throw off the servitude to French interests and return to German citizenship. The Nazis are trying to antedate their triumphant entry as the German power in the Saar.

The case of Austria, in which a strong Nazi movement exists and acknowledges Hitler as its leader, is grave. Sick to death financially, the fighting-ground of

Heimwehr reactionary country elements and the Socialists who rule in the city of Vienna, and threatened by Czechoslovakia's Triple Entente, and by Hungary, Austria should be helped by all and might be saved, if peace, internal and external, conciliation with freer trade and sound finance could be adopted as her conditions. Austria wants the *Anschluss*, the union with Germany which would in a peaceful Europe be safe and sound. The Nazi determination to possess Austria as part of the German Reich is at present inopportune. Here, as in Danzig and the Saar, German discontent and Nazi aspirations might combine to ignite dangerously.

UNIFICATION OF THE REICH

Foremost and fundamental among the changes which Hitler has effected is the Unification of the restored Reich. One of the first lessons of German History is how the multitude of petty principalities for centuries deprived the German race of any cohesion or unity as a great Imperial Power. The Holy Roman Empire realized by Charlemagne (The First Reich) degenerated into one of the titles of the Hapsburg Dynasty in Vienna; Frederick the Great in the eighteenth century raised Prussia to the leadership of the German States; Bismarck at the end of the nineteenth century used the victory over France to renew the German Empire (The Second Reich); early in the twentieth century the revenge of France, supported, as the Nazis devoutly believe, by "November Criminals," Pacifists and Jews, destroyed it; now in 1933 the

Empire (The Third Reich) has been more firmly than ever restored by Adolf Hitler. Charlemagne, Bismarck and Hitler . . . these three, and the greatest of them is Hitler! There is some truth in this . . . at least for Germans . . . and its meaning for the future cannot be denied.

Hitler has really put the Unification of the German Empire into practice in the two first months of his Dictatorship by his two Unification laws (April 13 and 15, 1933). In effect, Hitler now appoints the *Statthalter* in Bavaria, Saxony and all the States, which formed the Confederation of Germany; these *Statthalters* are Hitler's lieutenants in the absolute power Hitler wields, his decrees and control, the means and methods employed in his plans and policy have not to be adopted by the particular States; these had their privileges and peculiar ways, which limited and weakened central authority. The retirement of proud provincial rulers was quickly effected, as in Bavaria, where the Prime Minister, Dr. Held, a Reactionary Loyalist, in no sense a Marxist, was beaten by Brown Shirts; he soon made way for General von Epp, the Nazi ruler. Looking at this Revolutionary change, which has been effected with surprising efficiency, and welcoming the Unification of the Empire, Germans, who do not know, or care, what happens to Social-Democrats, pacifists and Jews, are in their way quite truthful, in saying that never was such a constitutional Revolution so bloodlessly concluded.

HOHENZOLLERN MONARCHY LESS LIKELY

This Unification is a new fact which Europe as yet fails to grasp. It makes the return of the Hohenzollerns, and certainly of the Kaiser, much less probable. The Kaiser left Germany on November 9, 1918, and has been waiting at Doorn, in Holland, for recall, hoping that the monarchist and reactionary forces would in time restore him. Hitler's progress and abuse of the Republic, and his alliance with the monarchist Nationalists to gain a majority of the Reichstag, may have made a restoration of the monarchy seem near. But Hitler never praised or defended the Kaiser; he abused and hated the men who tried to rule when the Kaiser fled; he said he would execute these criminals without trial; he never said he wanted the Kaiser brought back; what he wanted was the Third Reich established, and himself as its Leader (Führer).

His repeated assurance that much work awaited him and his Nation before they could consider the question of a Monarchy, was quite true and quite sensible. If a puppet King or a quiet compliant gentleman like the King of Italy were at hand and would give dignity and appearance of legality with the adhesion of the old aristocracy to his Dictatorship, Hitler might have spoken differently about a restoration of the Monarchy.

RETURN OF REIGNING PRINCES UNLIKELY

Unification of the Empire has a further result, which many have overlooked. It has changed the prospects for the Royal and Princely Families of Bavaria, Baden, Saxony and the smaller States. The Bavarians would not have submitted to the restoration of the Hohenzollern Emperor and King of Prussia, unless the Wittelsbach King of Bavaria had been restored in Munich. The Ruling Princes all fell together with the Kaiser; they would all have been restored with his return. Many of them had strong personal and popular claims. They were supported by circles of ancient titled and Junker families; the hereditary and class privileged in army, navy, diplomatic services and many other ways have been far too much continued by the Republic; from this aristocratic burden Hitler has relieved his Nation. To attempt to restore Kaiser without Ruling Princes and Junker power is not now practical politics.

LAND POLICY

The Agriculturists of Germany, whether great Landlords, especially those East of the Elbe, or peasant proprietors, or workers on the land,

have never been democrats or socialistically
inclined. Hitler early made a bid for agricultural support with an attractive list of
promises. His success in getting peasants and
land-workers to flock to him accounted much
for his increased votes since 1931. Agricultural
Policy is defined by the Party Programme and
in a Manifesto to Agriculturalists of all classes.
Remission of taxes, reduction of rates of
interest, land courts, summary action against
extortion, fixed prices to prevent market
speculation, transference of middlemen's businesses to agricultural associations, improved
conditions of living and wages for labourers,
prohibition of foreign labourers, state land-
colonies, agricultural schools with free places—
are among the promises. Of course, also,
increased protection against food supplies
coming in cheap from abroad; and the army
supplies to be generous to the men and well
paid for. There are said to be over two million
agricultural holdings in Germany and about
three million small holdings and allotments;
22 per cent. of the German people live on the
land and over thirteen and a half millions
directly depend on it for subsistence; a very
great proportion of these are in financial straits
and the promise of freedom from Interest-
Thraldom (Zinsenknechtshaft) is a grand
prospect. Hitler's sincere intention for the
land-workers must not be doubted.

HITLER'S SOCIALISM

The Labour Policy of Germany is clearly
going to follow the lines of Fascist Italy and
the Corporate State. There will be no freedom,
no popular democratic ownership or self-
government within the labour organization
and a diminished amount of freedom for the
Capitalist entrepreneur and employer. Hitler's
Programme lays great stress on two Points:
The Common Interest before Self as the Spirit
of the Programme; Abolition of the Thraldom
of Interest as the Core of National Socialism.

The first thing to realize about the Labour
Policy of Hitler is that it is Socialist and
anti-Capitalist. His Socialism is as thorough
and emphatic as the strongest Internationalist
Marxian could desire: thus in his Programme:

"The three main obstacles to carrying out National
Socialism are Marxism, the Parliamentary system and
the Capitalist Magnates. . . . Our Campaign against
Mammon, the world-embracing power of money, the
perpetual exploitation of our Nation by the great
lending houses. . . . Money-lenders, profiteers, banks,
financiers supply no necessity, instead they draw huge
profits from the prevailing system . . ." and "A limit
shall be set to the amassing of wealth in the hands of
individuals." "An obligational year of Labour or service for every German . . . will show the blessing of the
strict fulfilment of duty in working for the service of
the Nation."

NO TRADES UNIONS ALLOWED

Of course, the sacred nature of private property, the liberty of a man to work where he chooses, the offer of profit-sharing, and the great extension of health insurance and pensions for aged workers are in the picture. But the State is parent and partner; Hitler is not only the Saviour of the Nation, but also the succourer of the worker. With such sentiments he may have persuaded himself of this noble-mindedness when on May 2, 1933 he sent hundreds of Nazis to surround the offices of the great Trades Unions.

The great Nazi coup was threatened and expected; it was none the less a mean tyrannical deed to raid and rob the great trade organizations . . . with about ten million members in all . . . Free Unions, the Christian (Catholic) Unions, the Unions in close alliance with the Social-Democrat Party. They had politically acquiesced when their political leaders, their press and activities were suppressed, hoping to retain their existence and their funds; now their offices were raided, their officials imprisoned, and their funds confiscated.

The alleged justification for the strong measures taken is that there has been gross corruption and embezzlement; their crime was that they voted sums to establish play-

grounds, rest-homes, Institutes, etc., and con-
tributions to party campaign funds, and
Reichsbanner for processions, flags and uniforms—in a word, they used their funds in
party politics against the Brown Shirt bullies.
For that their leaders in prison will be driven
to suicide, or sentenced to long years of
imprisonment. Hitler made all this so clear
with eloquence at the First Congress of
National Labour; he has confiscated the funds
and property of the Unions in order to com-
pensate the workers for the losses caused by
their fraudulent leaders' robberies. The
confiscations of funds, buildings and properties,
including People's Houses (Volkshäuser),
Vorwärts Building, Co-operative Stores, etc.,
amount to many millions of Reichsmarks.
Hitler's speech, wonderfully attuned to the
occasion, appeared in every paper and is
sounded on every wireless set, but neither
printed paper nor human voice may utter a
word for the accused trades-unionists. Hitler's
speech on the occasion may be remembered:

From to-day there will be no Marxist Unions. Hence-
forth there will be only one Trade Union . . . the
German Worker. . . . I have taken a holy oath, to
destroy Marxism. I shall continue this task methodically
and without mercy. We have not taken reprisals. If we
had, we should have slain tens of thousands of them. . . .
I am no friend of titles; on my gravestone I want nothing
more than my name. My singular career has enabled
me to understand and comprehend the life of the whole

German family; destiny cast me down among these broad masses; I once earned my bread myself on the scaffolding; I stood for years among the masses as a simple German soldier. . . . Destiny has chosen me to be an honest broker for all. . . . I shall know no greater pride in life than to be able at the end of my days to say "I won the German Reich for the German Workman" (*The Times*, May 11, 1933).

RELIGION AND ART

Religion and Art are to be used and moulded in the National-Socialist State. Roman-Catholicism is international and pacific, and at present increasingly generous and tolerant. This is not in tune with Hitler's methods. The Roman Catholic Bishops of Bavaria have been among the very few able, and daring, to raise their voices against Nazi cruelty.

The leading Nazi persons, Göring, Goebbels, Feder and Rosenberg, are reputed Catholics, as well as Hitler; a *modus vivendi* between Catholic and Nazi may be found.

The Protestantism of Germany has suffered from divisions between Lutheran and Reformed (Calvinist) and among the various Provincial Churches (Landeskirchen); this has weakened Protestantism as a national force; and the great theological divergences, the radical, mediating and strong-orthodox schools, have complicated matters; attempts at union and federation have had some success. Now with a new spirit for a united "Front" there is a prospect of a United Protestant German Church, which of course will be inspired by Hitler's ideals.

Art is not to be neglected nor left untouched by the Nazis. They have made a boast of ridding the press, the theatres and public resorts of indecency and have restrained unbecoming manners and exiguity of dress in bathing-resorts and elsewhere.

Moreover they have purged the stages, picture-shows, opera and concert perform-.ances of the presence of Jewish artists and producers. Max Reinhardt, Bruno Walter, and many other artists of the first rank, until four months ago acclaimed as leaders of German culture, have been outcast. Performances may have artistically deteriorated. But the German can now find in them a "pure delight."

Pictorial Propaganda, Press Illustration and Poster Novelty are conspicuously admirable in Germany to-day. Much is being done by Nazi energy to control and mould them to National ends.

HEALTH AND RACE PURITY

A systematic effort to improve the health and bodily strength of the German population is foreshadowed; not merely by school children's health sheets and work arising therefrom, but working upwards the health and condition of civil servants, students and progressively of the whole population will come under review. The Race Office will deal with new legislation proposed to preserve the perfect purity of the Nordic race by various provisions; separation of the races; prohibition of marriages between different races; the segregation of persons whose offspring is undesirable; voluntary and advised, or even compulsory, sterilization is likely to come later. Until recently Berlin had matrimonial advice offices and other medical publicly supported agencies (V.D. cases, etc.): these have all been closed pending new arrangements which "will harmonize with the new ideals of the Government in this sphere."

SPORT

Sport has been one of the directions in which Germany since 1918 has made immense and healthy progress. Young men and girls have learned our British games; Football and Tennis, Golf, Hockey and other games have been taken up in Germany (as indeed in most European lands) with splendid enthusiasm. A good sporting spirit has been shown in International contests and tournaments, team tours, etc. This has been partly due to the absence of military exercising from the Schools of the Republic and to the abeyance of Conscription. In future, military exercises are to be introduced as early as possible; games are to have less attention so that military exercises and army drill may be taught; in the year of compulsory labour service, which will be inaugurated from December 1, 1933, military discipline will be introduced. *Wehrsport* (Military exercises and games) will be a daily task in schools, camps, and prisons.

NO JEWS IN "NATIONAL" SPORT

Sport will be controlled in every possible way for the Nazi ideals; and pure sport as play and recreation must suffer. On April 24, 1933, Jewish Lawn Tennis Players were by an Edict debarred from playing in International Matches in Germany; Official Championships, and inter-club fixtures; Jews may not serve on the Committee of any club affiliated to the German Lawn Tennis Association nor represent Germany in the Davis Cup Team; and the State Commissioner of each locality was to shortly settle definitely further restrictions. This decree debars Germany's best Lawn Tennis player, Dr. Daniel Prenn, a Jew of Russian origin, from playing as a German in any international match.

Following on this is announced the death by suicide of one of the famous women Lawn Tennis Players of Germany, Frau Nelly Neppach, who as a Jewish national ends her seven years of Woman Championship as an outcast from any Club affiliated to the German Lawn Tennis Association.

EDUCATION POLICY

The Education Policy and the changes in the Universities at once inaugurated by Hitler's Ministers show the vast change of direction which has come to German culture. Not only have scores of teachers been dismissed as Jews or Marxists and the methods and atmosphere altered, but the root idea that Education was to develop freely what powers lay in the individual and to strengthen intellectual and moral independence has been rejected. Dr. Frick, Nazi Minister of the Interior, at a Conference in Berlin made this clear.

Dr. Frick said the dominant principle was now to be service to, and identity with, the State, not the liberal theory of individual thought; the youth must be taught that he is one of the 100,000,000 German family, a third of whom are outside the frontiers; he must be reared to a readiness to bear arms, and to do the will, not of his parents, but of the State. New history books would be used, showing the heroic struggle of the nation against a world of foes, the humiliation through the Versailles "dictate" . . . and so on to the break through of their bonds to the National-Socialist ideal of freedom and reconstruction.

It will be observed that as the German nation now numbers 60,000,000, the 100,000,000 of this Pan-German aim assumes that Alsace-Lorraine, the Tyrol and Austria, and also Holland and the Scandinavian countries, with other "outside Germans" must be included so as to bring the whole German nation to German soil, which shall one day reach from Arctic to the Alps. This fantastic megalomania, though not yet found in Hitler's speeches, is apparently to be taught to children in the schools!

UNIVERSITIES UNDER HITLER

The Universities of Germany have been famous for generations as homes of leading learned men and societies, open to foreign students and scholars, ready to consider and test discoveries and theories, wonderfully equipped with laboratories, hospitals, libraries, and Institutions. Some have had proud claims; at Könisberg, the lifelong home of Immanuel Kant, it was impossible to forget the author of his classic *On Eternal Peace*; Göttingen University was founded by an English King and Britons have always been welcome students there. In recent years the interchange of both teachers and students between German Universities and Universities in U.S.A. and Britain have been mutually welcome. In the space of three months the picture of German Universities as homes of civilization and science is changed into one of turbulent hot-headed Nazi youths, whose Leader has turned out of their Professorships the best teachers because they were Jews or not sufficiently devoted to the National resurrection.

In every University there has been established by Hitler a Studenthood (Studentenschaft); to such a privileged assembly of students are entrusted powers never given before to any body of immature scholars. They superintend the admission of new students, can, and indeed they will, insist on unbending loyalty to Hitler, and see that only one Jewish student is admitted for every hundred German students; the Jews in Germany being less than one per cent. of the German population, i.e. before the exodus and "extermination" of the Jews began in February

1933; this dangerous proportion must be carefully guarded!

Professors may now be reported to the Minister for removals at the request of the Studenthood. Such removal of eminent men has occurred in large numbers. Difficulties caused by Nazi students led to the resignation of Dr. Kohlrausch, the Rector of Berlin University. The *Manchester Guardian* of May 13 printed a list of just 200 Professors and High School (Hoch-Schulen) Teachers who had been retired as Jews, or otherwise out of agreement with the "revived National Spirit." The dismissal of the most competent teachers is so serious, and the new teachers in their places so inferior, that standard of learning, dignity and discipline have grievously suffered in German Universities.

HOLOCAUST OF NON-GERMAN BOOKS

Even more astonishing is the students' destruction of thousands of books, which have been taken, apparently without either authority from the Government or protest from the custodians, from Public and Private Libraries. All books written by Jews (presumably therefore works by Heine or Spinoza), and books by Pacifists (and if so, would the works of Kant be taken?), works showing the horrors and illusions of war, and works in any way "repugnant to the national feelings," books scientific, medical and legal, books of admitted authority and works of reference, the books of Dr. Hirschfeld, a world-wide medical authority, taken *en masse* from his famous Institute, with a bust of himself, all these collected on May 10, 1933, and taken to a huge bonfire in the Opera Square. Here all were solemnly burnt. Dr. Goebbels presided. The searchlights and wireless installations made the event a grand public sensation. Similar public burning of books by students have taken place in other University towns. To give opportunities for patriotic reading complete sets of books by Nazi authors and many copies of Hitler's *My Struggle* have been donated to those public libraries which have given up books to be burnt. These doings are so amazing to many lovers of Pre-Hitler Germany that they say "Well, it is hard to believe, and quite impossible to approve, what seems to be absolute fact."

LEGAL RIGHTS AND PROCEDURE

The extent to which the whole idea and practice of law, justice administration and legal procedure have been swept aside is without parallel in recent times. Decrees are issued to take immediate effect everywhere, and applicable though no notice or warning has been given to the general public. Police, including "auxiliary police," which means in effect any S.A., S.S. or Brown-Shirt detachment, have the right to enter any business premises or dwellings at any hour, to close any office or shop, to remove or confiscate any property, to apprehend, remove and imprison any person on suspicion, or to prevent any undesirable event or action to or by any person, to put businesses, shops, factories or offices into the control of other, or unexperienced, persons or agents —all these powers freely exercised make a legal basis of society impossible and superfluous.

Not every citizen, not even more than a minority, suffers immediately under these conditions. In the general enthusiasm and belief that Germany is "born again," things are accepted which will not always be endured. It is serious when Courts of Law are degraded into becoming not homes of justice but, as in Moscow, avowed organs of State policy.

NO "OBJECTIVITY OR EQUALITY BEFORE THE LAW"

The Higher Provincial Court (Oberlandsgericht) at Frankfurt, has seen its Presiding Judge Heldtmann, a strong Nationalist, superseded for refusing to administer Nazi Justice. The new Ministerial Director Freisler, speaking to the assembled Court, said that "objectivity and equality before the law were no longer to be recognized nor allowed; these were liberal illusions and now quite superfluous; we have to establish the new State order." One result is the literally hundreds of "corruption trials," supported by perverted evidence, and pressed on, while the famous Lahusen case, involving Nazi Party supporters, is repeatedly postponed.

AUTHOR'S EPILOGUE

THE Hitler Revolution and the ending of Germany's Weimar Republic by the Nazi Dictatorship are here brought down to May 17, 1933. On that day Hitler made in the Reichstag his reply to the challenging offer from Roosevelt. Therein Hitler displayed his power in eloquence, elevated tone, clear statement, strong appeal and fair promises. For these things the world, as well as his countrymen, can be thankful. All are encouraged to hope afresh that the Disarmament and World Economic Conferences will lead to World Peace and Recovery.

The question still remains and cannot be ignored—Can the Democracies of America, France and the British Empire live in close amity and mutual esteem with a Nation basing a grandiose Realm on the complete suppression of all freedom in Press, Speech or Criticism, on an Anti-Semitism of cruel fanaticism, and on military organization, education and objects? In a word, is Hitlerism compatible with the peaceful progress of civilization?

J. K.

TILFORD,
  May 18, 1933.

CPSIA information can be obtained
at www.ICGtesting.com
Printed in the USA
BVHW051011270223
659295BV00002B/91

9 781014 151971